Jeremiah

INTERFACES
Series Editor: Barbara Green, O.P.

Jeremiah

Preacher of Grace, Poet of Truth

Carol J. Dempsey, OP

A Michael Glazier Book

LITURGICAL PRESS
Collegeville, Minnesota

www.litpress.org

A Michael Glazier Book published by Liturgical Press

Cover design by Ann Blattner. Watercolor by Ethel Boyle.

1	2	3	4	5	6	7	8

Library of Congress Cataloging-in-Publication Data

Dempsey, Carol J.
    Jeremiah : preacher of grace, poet of truth / Carol J. Dempsey.
      p. cm. — (Interfaces)
    "A Michael Glazier book."
    Includes bibliographical references.
    ISBN-13: 978-0-8146-5985-4 (alk. paper)
      1. Jeremiah (Biblical prophet) 2. Bible. O.T. Jeremiah—Criticism, interpretation, etc. I. Title. II. Series: Interfaces (Collegeville, Minn.)

BS580.J4D46   2006
224'.2092—dc22

                                               2006012312

To Ben Asen

who first awakened the prophetic spirit within me

To Bob Vaughn, OP

who helped to free that spirit

and

To my students of many years

for whom this book is written

CONTENTS

PREFACE

The book you hold in your hand is one of fifteen volumes in an expanding set of volumes. This series, called INTERFACES, is a curriculum adventure, a creative opportunity in teaching and learning, presented at this moment in the long story of how the Bible has been studied, interpreted, and appropriated.

The INTERFACES project was prompted by a number of experiences that you, perhaps, share. When I first taught undergraduates, the college had just received a substantial grant from the National Endowment for the Humanities, and one of the recurring courses designed within the grant was called Great Figures in Pursuit of Excellence. Three courses would be taught, each centering on a figure from some academic discipline or other, with a common seminar section to provide occasion for some integration. Some triads were more successful than others, as you might imagine. But the opportunity to concentrate on a single individual—whether historical or literary—to team teach, to make links to another pair of figures, and to learn new things about other disciplines was stimulating and fun for all involved. A second experience that gave rise to this series came at the same time, connected as well with undergraduates. It was my frequent experience to have Roman Catholic students feel quite put out about taking "more" biblical studies, since, as they confidently affirmed, they had already been there many times and done it all. That was, of course, not true; as we well know, there is always more to learn. And often those who felt most informed were the least likely to take on new information when offered it.

A stimulus as primary as my experience with students was the familiarity of listening to friends and colleagues at professional meetings talking about the research that excites us most. I often wondered: Do her undergraduate students know about this? Or how does he bring these ideas—clearly so energizing to him—into the college classroom? Perhaps some of us have felt bored with classes that seem wholly unrelated to research, that rehash the same familiar material repeatedly. Hence the idea for this series of books to bring to the fore and combine some of our research interests with our teaching and learning. Accordingly, this series is not so much about creating texts *for* student audiences but rather about *sharing* our scholarly passions with them. Because these volumes are intended each as a piece of original scholarship, they are geared to be stimulating to both students and established scholars, perhaps resulting in some fruitful collaborative learning adventures.

The series also developed from a widely shared sense that all academic fields are expanding and exploding, and that to contemplate "covering" even a testament (let alone the whole Bible or western monotheistic religions) needs to be abandoned in favor of something with greater depth and fresh focus. At the same time, the links between our fields are becoming increasingly obvious as well, and the possibilities for study which draw together academic realms that had once seemed separate is exciting. Finally, the spark of enthusiasm that almost always ignited when I mentioned to students and colleagues the idea of single figures in combination—interfacing—encouraged me that this was an idea worth trying.

And so with the leadership and help of Liturgical Press Academic Editor Linda Maloney, as well as with the encouragement and support of Editorial Director Mark Twomey, the series has begun to take shape.

Each volume in the INTERFACES series focuses clearly on a biblical character (or perhaps a pair of them). The characters from the first set of volumes are in some cases powerful—King Saul, Pontius Pilate—and familiar—John the Baptist, Jeremiah; in other cases they will strike you as minor and little-known—the Cannibal Mothers, Herodias. The second "litter" I added notables of various ranks and classes: Jezebel, queen of the Northern Israelite realm; James of Jerusalem and "brother of the Lord"; Simon the Pharisee, dinner host to Jesus; Legion, the Gerasene demoniac encountered so dramatically by Jesus. In a third set we find a similar contract between apparently mighty and marginal characters: Jezebel's husband Ahab, king of Israel; the prophet Jonah who speaks a few powerfully efficacious words; and Ben Sira, sage in late second temple Judah; and less powerful but perhaps an even greater reading challenge stand Jephthah's daughter and Ezekiel's wife. The fourth cluster features the prophet Jeremiah, the northern king Ahab, and the apostle Peter. In any case, each of them has been chosen to open up a set of worlds for consideration. The named (or unnamed) character interfaces with his or her historical-cultural world and its many issues, with other characters from biblical literature; each character has drawn forth the creativity of the author, who has taken on the challenge of engaging many readers. The books are designed for college students (though we think suitable for seminary courses and for serious Bible study), planned to provide young adults with relevant information and at a level of critical sophistication that matches the rest of the undergraduate curriculum.

In fact, the expectation is that what students are learning in other classes of historiography, literary theory, and cultural anthropology will find an echo in these books, each of which is explicit about at least two relevant methodologies. It is surely the case that biblical studies is in a methodology-conscious moment, and the INTERFACES series embraces it enthusiastically. Our hope is for students to continue to see the relationship between their best questions and their most valuable insights, between how they approach texts and what they find there. The volumes go well beyond familiar paraphrase of narratives to ask questions that are relevant in our era. At the same time, the series authors also have each dealt with the notion of the Bible as Scripture in a way condign for them. None of the books is preachy or hortatory, and yet the self-implicating aspects of working with the revelatory text are handled frankly. The assumption is, again, that college can be a good time for people to reexamine and rethink their beliefs and assumptions, and they need to do so in good company.

The INTERFACES volumes all challenge teachers to revision radically the scope of a course, to allow the many connections among characters to serve as its warp and weft. What would emerge fresh if a Deuteronomistic History class were organized around King Saul, Queen Jezebel, and the two women who petitioned their nameless monarch? How is Jesus' ministry thrown into fresh relief when structured by shared concerns implied by a demoniac, a Pharisee, James—a disciple and John the Baptist—a mentor? And for those who must "do it all" in one semester, a study of Genesis' Joseph, Herodias and Pontius Pilate might allow for a timely foray into postcolonialism. With whom would you now place the long-suffering but doughty wife of Ezekiel: with the able Jezebel, or with the apparently celibate Jonah? Or perhaps with Herodias? Would Jephthah's daughter organize an excellent course with the Cannibal Mothers, and perhaps as well with the Gerasene demoniac, as fresh and under-heard voices speak their words to the powerful? Would you study monarchy effectively by working with bluebloods Ahab and Saul, as they contend with their opponents, whether John the Baptist, Peter, or Pontius Pilate? What words of consolation and alarm might Jeremiah offer? Depending on the needs of your courses and students, these rich and diverse character studies will offer you many options.

The INTERFACES volumes are not substitutes for the Bible. In every case, they are to be read with the text. Quoting has been kept to a minimum, for that very reason. The series is accompanied by a straightforward companion, *From Earth's Creation* to John's *Revelation: The INTERFACES Biblical Storyline Companion,* which provides a quick overview of the whole storyline into which the characters under special study fit. The companion is available gratis for those using two or more of the INTERFACES volumes. Already readers of diverse proficiency and familiarity have registered satisfaction with this slim overview narrated by biblical Sophia.

The series challenge—for publisher, writers, teachers, and students—is to combine the volumes creatively, to INTERFACE them well so that the vast potential of the biblical text continues to unfold for us all. These volumes offer a foretaste of other volumes currently on the drawing board. It has been a pleasure to work with the authors of these volumes as well as with the series consultants: Carleen Mandolfo for Hebrew Bible and Catherine Murphy for New Testament. It is the hope of all of us that you will find the series useful and stimulating for your own teaching and learning.

Barbara Green, O.P.
INTERFACES Series Editor
May 16, 2006
Berkeley, California

ACKNOWLEDGMENTS

This volume would not have been possible without the support of colleagues and friends who have given generously of their time and effort, gifts and talents. I would like to express my thanks to the library staff at the University of Portland, in particular Vickie Hamilton and Caroline Mann, who obtained for me the research material I needed to write this volume. I would also like to thank Catherine Dodt, a theology major who graduated from the University. Katie spent countless summer hours typing this manuscript and providing me with insightful comments "from the point of view of a student," for whom the volumes in the Interfaces series are written. Special thanks is also extended to Elizabeth Michael Boyle, O.P., who helped with the typing of the indices.

I would also like to thank Linda M. Maloney, academic editor of the Liturgical Press, who has supported this project most enthusiastically. Linda's wonderful humor, her constant encouragement and willingness to consult at various stages of this project, and above all her untiring patience in waiting for me to finish this project have indeed been a blessing. Linda, thank you.

Last, I would like to express my deepest gratitude to Barbara Green, O.P., Interfaces series editor, for her vision, patience, and persistence in bringing this whole project to birth. Throughout my writing of this manuscript Barbara has offered me many critical comments and has raised excellent questions in an effort to make the volume the best it can be. Barbara's insight and astute hearing of the text are without measure. As my colleague she has given me more intellectual challenges than could be handled in this single volume. As my Dominican sister and friend she has been most supportive of my efforts as we try together to be faithful to our Order's charism of the intellectual life and preaching. To you, Barbara, I owe a heartfelt debt of gratitude for inviting me to be a part of your wonderful project. Thank you.

INTRODUCTION AND
INTERSECTIONS
Encountering Jeremiah

Now the word of the Lord came to me saying,
Before I formed you in the womb
   I knew you
And before you were born
   I consecrated you;
I appointed you
   A prophet to the nations. (Jer 4:1)

Perhaps no other prophet in the Bible is as complex and developed as Jeremiah, a poet of grace and a prophet *par excellence* who knew, first hand, the bittersweet experience of what it means to be madly in love with God and madly in love with God's people. Such a wildly compelling and intimate love is at the heart of Jeremiah's prophetic vocation. This great and deep love sustains, energizes, and empowers Jeremiah even when he is faced with relentless adversity, cruel rejection, and unjust oppression, all of which would have cost him his life had it not been for the wonderful promise given to him by God at the beginning of his divine call and commission: "I will be with you . . . to deliver you" (1:19). This promise remains steadfast in Jeremiah's life and becomes a sacred reminder of God's presence to him and to the people, even under the most horrible of circumstances when Judah is ravaged, the holy city Jerusalem destroyed, the Temple burned, and the remnant of his people scattered. For the people of his day, and certainly for people today, Jeremiah—as a survivor of such tragedies—becomes a living symbol of God's enduring promise to be faithful to the ancient covenants made with Abraham, Sarah, Isaac, Rebekkah, Jacob, Rachel, Leah, Moses, and David. Just as Jeremiah lives on, so will God's people, in spite of their experience of great pain, suffering, and loss.

This study, as a contribution to the series INTERFACES, focuses on Jeremiah as a literary character in the book of Jeremiah to (a) determine how his character evolves and develops through (1) what he says, (2) what he does, (3) what he experiences, (4) how he interacts with other characters in the text, (5) how he interacts with God, and (6) how he interacts with the social, political, and religious situation of his day; and to (b) present Jeremiah as a gifted and skilled preacher whose rhetoric is poetic, passionate, and prophetic. The biblical texts used throughout the study are taken from the New Revised Standard Version of the Bible.

Because a prophet is informed by and responds to his or her historical times and social location, this study sketches the historical dimensions of Jeremiah's times as they pertain to his character, its development, and the work he must do on behalf of his God and God's people. The study employs in detail the art of rhetorical criticism as well as narrative criticism when necessary, to shed light on Jeremiah as a primary actor in the book of Jeremiah. A focus on the use of various rhetorical forms—imagery, symbolism, metaphor, simile, the use of the vocative, among others—is included in the study of each chapter's texts. Also highlighted is the role imagination plays in Jeremiah's religious experience, and how imaginative religious experience finds its way into Jeremiah's proclamations that become prophetic for his hearers. The study is a synchronic treatment of the Jeremiah material, and one that is text and reader-centered. Finally, the study has a hermeneutical dimension to it that raises questions for continued thought while bringing to the fore various points held up for critical theological and ethical reflection. Thus this study "interfaces" on several levels and in several ways, and includes to some extent an "interface" with the prophetic tradition as well.

Seven chapters and an epilogue comprise this study. Chapter 1, "'Now the Word of the Lord Came to Me . . .': A Poet Graced, A Prophet Afflicted," begins with a detailed study of Jeremiah 1:4-10, which becomes the cornerstone text for the entire discussion that follows in this first and subsequent chapters. The chapter focuses on Jeremiah as the one graced by God and having a mission and word that are deeply personal and profoundly repugnant to his audience.

Chapter 2, "'Declare This in the House of Jacob . . .': A Portrait of Uncompromising Fidelity," features Jeremiah fulfilling the mission ordained by God: he proclaims what God has told him to say and performs certain actions God has commanded him to do. Jeremiah's fidelity to God is the focal point of the chapter. Selected texts also highlight the religious imagination of Jeremiah and the role imagination plays in the prophetic tradition as embodied by him. The breadth of Jeremiah's mission becomes clear through passages that feature him addressing not only the house of Judah but also other nations. His proclamations of woe and comfort attest to the justice and compassion of God, and feature Jeremiah as God's poet of chaos and comfort. The chapter focuses on Jeremiah faithfully delivering God's word and doing what God asks him to do, and boldly proclaiming the divine word of woe to Judah and other nations, though it is not the prophet's final word to them. Rather, the final word offered is one of divine comfort and promised restoration.

Chapter 3, "Gussied in Loincloth and Sporting a Yoke: Symbols Come to Life," continues a theme introduced in chapter 2, specifically the theme of symbolic gesture. This chapter features Jeremiah as one who willingly performs a series of symbolic actions commanded by God, the meaning of which God explains to Jeremiah. In this chapter readers see Jeremiah's life become the living embodiment of what is about to occur historically to his people and the kingdom of Judah.

The central focus of the series in which this study appears comes to light in chapter 4, "In Conversation with God." This chapter explores God "interfacing" with Jeremiah. Such "interfacing" sheds light not only on Jeremiah but also on Jeremiah's experience and perception of God.

The theme of "interfacing" continues in chapter 5, "Persistence and Courage in the Face of Opposition and Threat." Here Jeremiah "interfaces" with a variety of other characters present in the book. Such exchanges continue to elucidate Jeremiah's person and prophetic vocation and mission.

Chapter 6 portrays Jeremiah known to his God as a person of prayer who, in fact, is seen as one who prays to his God for understanding. This is perhaps the most intimate of all chapters in this study. Jeremiah's unreserved faith and trust in God stand in stark contrast to his people's idolatry and apostasy.

More than any other chapter in this study, the final chapter, "The Prophetic Paradox of Letting Go," focuses on the self-reflective language of Jeremiah, which reveals his inner struggles and pain as he moves from pathos to trust, from imprisonment to freedom, from desperation to conviction. The images of Jeremiah as a preacher of grace and a poet of truth—a prophet *par excellence*—converge in this chapter, suggesting to readers a sense of wonder and awe.

Finally, the Epilogue provides a brief summary, a few concluding remarks, and some implications for readers today. This last section of the study pulls together the character and personality of Jeremiah and suggests to readers how they, too, have the potential to be preachers of grace and poets of truth like Jeremiah, who did in fact live to see the world fall apart around him but whose own life became a living testimony to the enduring and sustaining presence of God whose work of redemption and transformation is never-ending.

Setting the Stage

Before delving into the study of the Jeremiah text itself, we will first give a basic overview of the historical times of Jeremiah, followed by a general introduction to the literary and theological content of the Jeremiah text as a whole, and then a brief comment on the character Jeremiah as a person, a prophet, and a poet.

Approaching the Character and Text of Jeremiah Methodologically

In order to gain insight into the character of Jeremiah and arrive at a holistic understanding of his person as a biblical figure within the prophetic tradition we need first to listen to the biblical text itself, especially to the voice of Jeremiah, whose various proclamations, lamentations, and symbolic gestures are all revelatory of his character, his world, his community, his experience and perception of God, and essentially of God. Woven throughout this study, then, is a historical perspective that takes into account those events that shaped the life, mission, ministry, and preaching of Jeremiah the character as reflected by the biblical text. Attention is also given to certain theological perspectives and influences embedded in the prophet's proclamations, all of which attest to the humanness of the sacred and inspired word of the prophet—a word that will forever be historically, culturally, socially, and theologically conditioned but that, at its core, has the power to transform by exposing, exhorting, encouraging, and envisioning.

Central to gaining knowledge about Jeremiah will be the use of rhetorical criticism, one approach among many biblical methods that focuses on the rhetoric of the biblical text, the function of that rhetoric, and the effects the rhetoric had on an audience in Jeremiah's time and has on subsequent audiences in later eras, including today. Since much of the book of Jeremiah is poetry and since the character Jeremiah is a preacher, rhetorical criticism is one method highly appropriate to the focus of this study and the task at hand.

One of the leading voices in rhetorical criticism has been that of Jack R. Lundbom,[1] who in turn acknowledges that this analytical method for the

---

[1] For a detailed discussion of rhetorical criticism as it pertains to the study of the book of Jeremiah see Jack R. Lundbom, *Jeremiah 1–20.* AB 21A (New York: Doubleday, 1999), especially 68–92; idem, *Jeremiah 21–36.* AB 21B (New York: Doubleday, 2004); idem, *Jeremiah 37–52.* AB 21C (New York: Doubleday, 2004); idem, *Jeremiah: A Study in Ancient Hebrew Rhetoric* (2nd ed. Winona Lake: Eisenbrauns, 1997). For additional discussion of rhetorical criticism with respect to the writings of the prophets in general, see also Phyllis

study of discourse was born on American soil more than seventy-five years ago and that he is following in the trail blazed by James Muilenburg. Lundbom's own discussion of rhetorical criticism, as well as his use of it in his study of the book of Jeremiah, informs the present work.

For those engaged in rhetorical criticism, three elements are primary: structure, style, and audience. A rhetorical critic's first task is to identify and delimit units of discourse within the text. Once isolated, these individual units are then defined according to the canons of ancient Hebrew rhetoric, and not categorized according to literary genres superimposed on the various units.[2] Thus one asks: Is this unit a confession? a proclamation? a prayer? a liturgy for cultic recitation? a letter? a proverb or parable? a memoir? an argument? a narrative? a vision? Following the delimitation of units and the classification of these units into rhetorical forms, the rhetorical critic next pays attention to the literary techniques embedded in the units themselves. These techniques include simile, metaphor, imagery, symbolism, chiasmus, rhetorical questions, particles, wordplays, accumulation, verbal irony, parallelism, merismus, paronomasia, and many more. Attention is also given to catchwords and keywords used within and throughout the rhetorical units. Finally, the rhetorical critic is concerned with the text's primary and later audiences. How might Jeremiah's listeners have heard his proclamations? How do people hear them today? What is the interplay between literary form and technique and Jeremiah's message, and the impact that message has on his present and later audiences with whom he interfaces? What does Jeremiah's rhetoric reveal about himself, his audience, and his God? All of these dimensions will come into play throughout this study.

Because a good portion of the Jeremiah material is prose, and because the book as a whole is a literary work, the use of narrative criticism is also germane to this study.[3] Complementing rhetorical criticism with its concern for the audience, narrative criticism considers who the real and implied readers might be. The narrative critic has an eye for the same information as the rhetorical critic but pays careful attention to such elements as point of view, characterization and character development, character traits, setting, conflict, and feelings that a character's actions and words can elicit from an audience, e.g., empathy, sympathy, antipathy.

Trible, *Rhetorical Criticism: Context, Method, and the Book of Jonah.* Guides to Biblical Scholarship (Minneapolis: Fortress Press, 1994), and Yehoshua Gitay, "Rhetorical Criticism and the Prophetic Discourse," *JSNT* 50 (1991) 13–24.

[2] For example: a lawsuit, a judgment statement, a call to repentance, etc.

[3] For further study of narrative criticism see Mark Allan Powell, *What Is Narrative Criticism?* Guides to Biblical Scholarship (Minneapolis: Fortress Press, 1990).

Both rhetorical and narrative criticism have within their treasuries the tools for unlocking the wondrous and mysterious person of the character Jeremiah, and still more: the impetus for unleashing a compelling vision and vocation needed for the ongoing transformation of the entire planet.

The Historical Times and Social World of Jeremiah

The period between 627 B.C.E. and approximately 581 B.C.E., when Jeremiah is said to have lived, was a time of political upheaval, social unrest, and religious turbulence. Two of the great world powers and archrivals were Assyria and Babylon, with Assyria being the stronger of the two during the earlier part of the period. Assyria ruled by terror, and one of its major achievements was the invasion of the Northern Kingdom of Israel, an event that led to the deportation of countless numbers of Israelites. The gradual realignment of world powers, however, resulted in the toppling of the Assyrian empire, an event that paved the way for the rise of Babylon in Assyria's place. Governed by King Nebuchadnezzar, this new superpower had a voracious appetite for expansion. Babylon became the greatest threat to Judah, the surviving kingdom in the land of Israel, a situation that evoked a profound and sustained response from Jeremiah as he repeatedly warned the Judahites about what was to be their great misfortune in the national arena—the fall of Jerusalem, the destruction of the Temple, and the loss of the entire Southern Kingdom—all of which did happen. Jeremiah's preaching reflected and was informed and influenced by these events, the details of which will now be unraveled in order to provide a more comprehensive view of the world into which Jeremiah was born and that later received his word of grace, his message of truth.

Before the death of Solomon, around 922 B.C.E., Israel was a united country, but when Solomon died the kingdom split into two rival states: Israel and Judah, known as the Northern and Southern Kingdoms respectively. The capital of Israel was Samaria; the capital of Judah was Jerusalem. These two separate kingdoms had military regimes of their own as well as two different governments and religious practices. Israel was the larger and wealthier of the two kingdoms, but both were invaded by imperial Egypt at different intervals during their history, and both battled with their neighbors —Israel with the Arameans and Moabites, and Judah with the Edomites.

In the eighth century B.C.E. Israel and Judah both prospered, until the latter half of the century when geopolitical and religious events gravely affected both kingdoms. At that time Assyria, under the rule of Tiglath-pileser III (745–727 B.C.E.), was one of the strongest empires in the region. Assyria sought to increase its power base through territorial expansion, overrunning small, less powerful, vulnerable nations. In order to protect themselves against Assyria many of the smaller nations attempted to form a coalition, a move led by Rezin of the Aramean state of Damascus and Pekah ben Remaliah, ruler of Israel (737–732 B.C.E.), who came into power after he had usurped the throne of Israel's previous king. Both Rezin and Pekah ben Remaliah wanted Judah to join the coalition, but Judah's king Ahaz (735–715 B.C.E.) refused in an attempt to maintain Judah's independence.

Ahaz's decision not to join the coalition was met with opposition and in 735–732 B.C.E. brought on the so-called Syro-Ephraimite crisis, with Israel and Damascus allied against Judah. The Southern Kingdom was invaded as Rezin and Pekah ben Remaliah plotted to overthrow Ahaz. With his land under siege and his throne threatened, Ahaz lost trust in God and appealed to Tiglath-pileser III for assistance, a move the prophet Isaiah strongly contested. In order to secure the Assyrian king's support Ahaz sent him a large gift (see 2 Kgs 16:7-8). In return, Tiglath-pileser III moved against the Syro-Ephraimite coalition and destroyed it, thwarting its attempt to seize Judah and depose Ahaz. Tiglath-pileser then marched into Israel, took control of the Israelite lands in Galilee and the Transjordan, turned them into three Assyrian provinces, and destroyed Damascus in 732 B.C.E. Under the royal rule of Hoshea (732–724 B.C.E.) Israel became a small vassal state subject to Assyria. Judah remained an Assyrian vassal state until Assyria itself collapsed.

Incorporation into Assyria's power base did not offer Judah a respite from its geopolitical problems, though the threat of complete annihilation by another country or countries was greatly reduced for a brief period of time. The price Judah had to send to Assyria for assistance, however, was steep. As a vassal state Judah had to pay tribute to Assyria, and Ahaz had to appear before Tiglath-pileser in Damascus and pay homage to Assyria's gods at a bronze altar there. Ahaz then had to set up a copy of this altar in Jerusalem's Temple (see 2 Kgs 16:10-15). For the Judahites the religious stipulations were costly, but the kingdom's submission to Tiglath-pileser at these early stages of Assyria's rise to power perhaps safeguarded Judah against what Israel would eventually experience—invasion by the Assyrians and total collapse as a kingdom.

Because of a renewed spirit of rebellion among the Israelites led by Hoshea, who sought the help of Egypt, Shalmaneser V (727–722 B.C.E.), Tiglath-pileser's successor, became enraged with his vassal. He marched into Israel, took Hoshea prisoner, and occupied the land except for the capital city of Samaria, which eventually fell in 722/1 B.C.E. Thus the Northern Kingdom came to an end as Sargon II (722–704 B.C.E.) succeeded Shalmaneser V as Assyria's new king.

Israel's downfall was most likely due to internal political instability; six kings had ruled within twenty-five years. According to the biblical text, however, the kingdom's demise is said to have stemmed from the people's social depravity and religious infidelities that involved the worship of other gods and forgetfulness of Yhwh and Yhwh's covenant. There were also countless violations of Torah, especially worship of the Canaanite fertility god Baal alongside Yhwh (see 2 Kgs 17:7-18). Torah called Israel to single-heartedness. The prophet Hosea railed repeatedly against these transgressions but met with little, if any, success. The people continued in their duplicitous ways until such ways led to their own downfall.

Judah was aware of Israel's vulnerable situation before Shalmaneser V and before God, knew of the consequences endured, yet followed a similar path, trusting in the false pretense of the Zion Tradition and the inviolability of Jerusalem. From the Judahites' perspective the Temple was God's dwelling place, Jerusalem was God's holy city, and they were part of God's chosen people. No harm could come to them, regardless of their deeds—or so they thought.

Ahaz's successor was his son Hezekiah (715–687 B.C.E.). Hezekiah tried to reverse his father's policy. Since Judah was suffering from widespread and all-pervasive apostasy during Ahaz's reign, Hezekiah's first order of business was to usher in a religious reform and to instill a sense of patriotism into the Judahites that, he hoped, would lead them to want to seek independence from Assyria. Under Hezekiah's leadership Judah experienced a sweeping reform that had widespread positive social impact as well, all of which was needed to deal with the internal injustices that also plagued the kingdom. While Sargon II reigned, Hezekiah made no attempt to rebel against Assyria. It should be noted that Assyria also had control of Egypt at this time, with Sargon II plotting to reconquer Babylon even though Babylon's king Merodach-baladan was holding out against Assyria's efforts to depose him. Sargon II's son Sennacherib (704–681 B.C.E.) succeeded him, and under Sennacherib's reign Hezekiah, king of the vassal state Judah, made his move. He refused to pay the required tribute to Assyria (see 2 Kgs 18:7), thus asserting Judah's independence.

Hezekiah joined a coalition against Sennacherib and Assyria and sent envoys to Egypt in an effort to negotiate a treaty with that country as well (see Isa 30:1-7; 31:1-3). Egypt was committed to acting against Assyria. Sennacherib organized his troops and crushed the coalition in 701 B.C.E. Judah could not withstand Assyria, did not gain its independence, and was forced to pay Assyria a heavily increased tribute (see 2 Kgs 18:9–19:37). Assyria then turned its attention to rebellious Babylon, which it succeeded in overpowering in 689 B.C.E.

In Judah, King Manasseh (687–642 B.C.E.) succeeded his father Hezekiah. Unlike his father, Manasseh led Judah into becoming a noble vassal state; Judah gave full submission to Assyria, which reached the zenith of its power during Manasseh's reign. Led by Sennacherib's successors Esarhaddon (681–669 B.C.E.) and Ashurbanipal (669–627 B.C.E.), Assyria invaded Egypt and destroyed its capital in 663 B.C.E. Manasseh, for his part, followed in the ways of his grandfather Ahaz, beginning with the recognition of Assyria's gods. Such recognition led to other religious changes initiated by Manasseh. These included the restoration of local shrines, tolerance of the fertility cult with its sacred prostitution in the Temple precincts (see 2 Kgs 21:4-7; Zeph 1:4-5), permission for human sacrifice to the god Molech (2 Kgs 21:6), the erection of Asherah, and the worship of Baal and other astral deities. Amon (642–640 B.C.E.), Manasseh's son and successor, followed his father's policies. During Amon's reign Assyria under Ashurbanipal began to decline in power. Amon was assassinated, and Manasseh's eight-year-old grandson, Josiah (640–609 B.C.E.), became king.

Assyria's decline in power eventually provided Josiah with an opportunity to seek, once again, Judah's independence from Assyria. Like Hezekiah, Josiah made sweeping reforms, which included reviving and renewing the covenant spirit and the Passover feast. During Josiah's reign, Jeremiah began his ministry as a prophet. Josiah's reform did not achieve its intended widespread success.

Ashuruballit II succeeded Ashurbanipal. Babylon, under Nabopolassar, revolted against the Assyrians from 626 to 612 B.C.E., when Nineveh was finally destroyed, leaving the Assyrians no option but to retreat to Haran. The Babylonians eventually overran Haran in 610 B.C.E., and the Assyrian empire came to an end. Josiah died tragically in 609 B.C.E. Judah fell under at least nominal control of Egypt, and Babylon became the new world power.

Jehoiakim (609–598 B.C.E.) succeeded Josiah and allowed the reforms to lapse. Pagan practices became widespread (see, e.g., Jer 7:16-18; 11:9-13); the people became dispirited once again and continued in their socially and morally corrupt ways (see, e.g., Jer 5:26-29; 7:1-15). In Babylon, Nabopolassar died and Nebuchadnezzar succeeded him. Jehoiakim, seeking independence from Egypt, seems to have transferred his allegiance to Nebuchadnezzar, thus making Judah a vassal state of Babylon (see 2 Kgs 24:1). Once again Judah's fortunes were in the hands of a powerful empire that, like Assyria, had ruthless and arrogant ambitions of its own. However, when Babylon launched an attack against Egypt and was not overwhelmingly victorious, Jehoiakim interpreted the situation as a sign of Babylon's weakness. He seized the opportunity to rebel against Babylon (see 2 Kgs 24:1). His rebellion was the beginning of the demise of Judah at the hands of the Babylonians.

In 598 B.C.E. Jehoiakim died as the Babylonians began their march into Judah. Jehoiakim's eighteen-year-old son, Jehoiachin, succeeded his father (2 Kgs 24:8), and his reign was less than three months old when Jerusalem surrendered to the Babylonians (March 16, 597 B.C.E.). Jehoiachin, his mother, several central officials, and a number of key citizens were exiled to Babylon. Zedekiah (597–587 B.C.E.) was put on the throne to replace Jehoiachin. Judah persisted in its rebellious spirit and its corrupt internal ways. Political and social strife as well as religious depravity left Judah in chaos and vulnerable to attack. Many Judahites still considered Jehoiachin their king, which undermined the authority of Zedekiah. Still rebellious against Babylon, Judah met its fate in July of 587 B.C.E. when the Babylonians breached Jerusalem's walls and took the city. Zedekiah and some of his soldiers fled, only to be captured by Nebuchadnezzar's forces. Zedekiah was brought before the Babylonian king, who executed Zedekiah's sons as Zedekiah watched. He then blinded Zedekiah and took him in chains to Babylon, where Zedekiah eventually died (2 Kgs 25:6-7; Jer 52:9-11). Shortly after that Nebuzaradan, one of Nebuchadnezzar's commanders, torched Jerusalem, leveled its walls, and destroyed its Temple. The Judahites were exiled to Babylon and Egypt, and the Southern Kingdom of Judah, like Israel before it, came to an end. The biblical character Jeremiah lived through the harrowing reigns of Josiah, Jehoiakim, Jehoiachin, and Zedekiah. He witnessed the fall of Jerusalem and the end of Judah, and was himself exiled to Egypt.

Jeremiah's preaching is to be understood against the background of all these events of the seventh and sixth centuries B.C.E. as well as some of what happened earlier to Israel in the eighth century B.C.E. Indeed, Jeremiah's task as a prophet was monumental and his vision almost surreal. True to his vocation, he remained faithful to his preaching, his vision, and his God, despite all odds and despite the eventual loss of everything for Judah, which he knew was inevitable. Furthermore, Jeremiah understood all these events as Judah's "just desserts" from God for its internal political, social, and religious depravity. One of Jeremiah's several rousing proclamations delivered at the Temple gate provides a glimpse into the situation of his community:

> For if you truly amend your ways and your doings, if you truly act justly one with another, if you do not oppress the alien, the orphan, and the widow, or shed innocent blood in this place, and if you do not go after other gods to your own hurt, then I will dwell with you in this place, in the land that I gave of old to your ancestors forever and ever. Here you are, trusting in deceptive words to no avail. Will you steal, murder, commit adultery, swear falsely, make offerings to Baal, and go after

other gods that you have not known, and then come and stand before me in this house, which is called by my name, and say, "We are safe!"— only to go on doing all these abominations? Has this house, which is called by my name, become a den of robbers in your sight? You know, I too am watching, says the LORD. (Jer 7:5-11)

God's chosen people, who had been called to holiness, abandoned their God, broke covenant, chose another path, and in doing so cast the die for their own future disastrous course. The rampant injustice, loss of integrity, and debilitating discord left a once strong and vibrant community splintered within and prey to the ravenous appetite of the world's strongest empire, which eventually gobbled them up.[4]

The Literary Dimensions of the Book of Jeremiah

The literary composition of Jeremiah has sparked a lively conversation among scholars for years. The most active controversy has been the prose-poetry debate, which tried to determine which type of material was "authentic Jeremiah." This debate led earlier scholars, e.g., Friedrich Giesebrecht (1894) to assume multiple sources in the text of Jeremiah.[5] This idea of sources is largely a moot point today, although the common rhetorical tradition shared by the book of Jeremiah, the book of Deuteronomy, and the Deuteronomistic History is still an area of inquiry among contemporary scholars. The text's portrayal of Jeremiah is also debated.

With respect to the book's overall structure, scholars' proposals vary. Common among the suggestions is that chapters 1–25 consist of a series of prophetic messages; chapters 26–33 contain a famous Temple speech (ch. 26), followed by a series of conflicts between true and false prophets (chs. 27–29), and the Book of Consolation (chs. 30–33). Chapters 34–45 are a narrative account of what happened to Jeremiah in the last days of Judah, up to his exile to Egypt.

As a work of literary artistry the book of Jeremiah is rich in rhetorical form and technique; it includes, among other forms, psalms of praise, petition,

---

[4] For further discussion of the historical and social world of Jeremiah see John Bright, *A History of Israel* (4th ed. Louisville: Westminster John Knox, 2000), especially 269–339; Walter Brueggemann, *To Pluck Up, To Tear Down: A Commentary on the Book of Jeremiah 1–25* (Grand Rapids: Eerdmans, 1988); Jack R. Lundbom, *Jeremiah 1–20*, especially 102–106; and Henry McKeating, *The Book of Jeremiah* (Peterborough: Epworth Press, 1999).

[5] In his commentary (*Jeremiah 1–20*, 57–101) Lundbom succinctly outlines the prose and poetry debate as well as other literary issues generic to the book of Jeremiah.

and thanksgiving, individual and communal laments, a letter, and a parable. Dialogues between God and Jeremiah and the speeches Jeremiah delivers to his community are often poignant, heart-wrenching, consciousness-stinging, and heart-warming. Perhaps no other book in the prophetic corpus contains as moving and dramatic a collection of speeches as is found in the so-called "confessions" or laments of Jeremiah, where the poet bares his heart to God and prays through the pain associated with his prophetic office and vocation. Many of the rhetorical forms and techniques reveal Jeremiah as a gifted and talented preacher who is able to appeal to the heart, mind, moral conscience, and religious imagination of his community who, after hearing his message, often failed to heed it.

Theological Themes in the Book of Jeremiah

The overall fabric of the book of Jeremiah consists of announcements of doom and proclamations of hope. To examine these texts closely is to discover that embedded in these speeches, as well as in the book as a whole, is Jeremiah's own theology and theological perspective, reflecting the influence of both the Exodus and Wisdom traditions as well as many of the concerns of earlier prophets. Jeremiah's God is the God of creation[6] who "knows" people, events, and what the future holds,[7] who "remembers" (Jer 2:2; 14:10), who "sees" and acts, who is perceived as a righteous judge (Jer 11:20) and merciful (Jer 3:12), and who can be overpowering (Jer 20:7).[8]

Central to the book of Jeremiah is "the word of the Lord." For Jeremiah, God's "word" is central to his vocation and his preaching. This divine word is powerful. It moves Jeremiah to proclaim weal and woe, hope and comfort. Uncontrollable and all-consuming, it leads Jeremiah to an awareness of what is and a consciousness of what will be.

Two major themes that run through the book as a whole are sin-judgment and repentance-redemption-salvation. Embedded in these two themes is a theology of suffering. Jeremiah's community suffers because of its estrangement from God and its powerlessness in the face of an aggressive and powerful empire. This empire's charted course of conquest leads to destruction and exile. Consequently, the religious experience of Jeremiah's people, in the wake of such a horrific life experience, is nothing less than the excruciating pain that comes from the perception that, indeed, the God of Israel who had

---

[6] See, e.g., Jer 5:22, 24; 14:22; 27:5.

[7] See, e.g., Jer 1:5; 12:3; 15:15; 18:23; 29:11-23; 33:3.

[8] For further discussion of Jeremiah's experiences of God see Lundbom, *Jeremiah 1–20*, 144.

promised to remain faithful to the Israelite community has now, once and for all, abandoned the people. The rubble of the two kingdoms, described above, reflects the condition of the community: a heap of smoldering embers out of which will arise a spark to ignite the process of repentance, redemption, and restoration of the community, and the return of the community to its land.

As a member of his community, Jeremiah suffers because he sees the path his people have chosen. He is rebuffed and rebuked when he speaks out against their odious ways and choices. He bears not only the pain of the oppressed within the community, the pain of the impending and eventual loss of Judah, and the personal pain of having to do "the right thing" demanded by his prophetic vocation and office, but also the pain of God who agonizes over the people's infidelity and the tragedies that are about to befall them as a result of their internal strife and discord. And yet both Jeremiah the character and Jeremiah the book are essentially about a theology of hope, first expressed in Jeremiah 1:10:

> See, today I appoint you over nations and over kingdoms,
>> to pluck up and to pull down,
>> to destroy and to overthrow,
>> to build and to plant.

The newly emerging vision is contained within the leveling process of the old; exposure of infidelities and injustices provides the requisite fertilized terrain on which hope can once again spring eternal.

The Prophetic Persona and Jeremiah

In order to appreciate Jeremiah as a passionate, prophetic, and poetic preacher we need to know something about the prophetic persona and tradition Jeremiah so clearly embodies.

The prophet is one who is madly in love with God and God's people. Usually a very "ordinary" person, the prophet is often God's "surprise" to a group of people, presenting them with an unexpected word, insight, or vision that can either jar and cut to the quick or comfort, soothe, and salve a bleeding wound, a broken dream, a shattered life. Delivering God's word is never easy, and as Jack Lundbom observes, "the prophet has to be as hard as a rock even while [he is] being torn apart inside."[9] Thus to be prophetic

[9] Ibid.

and to embrace the prophetic tradition is to embrace and free that Spirit of God within the context of one's own life and in relation to one's sense of mission that is always divinely ordained.

As a vocation, the prophetic office and way of life are, together, a profound gift that demands a freedom of spirit and a willingness to let go to God. The vocation carries with it a responsibility to God, to God's people, and to God's creation. Often feeling a sense of reluctance about assuming and bearing this responsibility, a prophet is called not to be successful but to be faithful. Perhaps the greatest gift a prophet can give to a community is to become the living embodiment of God's Spirit. Thus a prophet becomes prophetic through his and her life and being, and not just through deeds. This integration of a prophet's being and work in the context of the prophetic tradition helps, then, to link the prophet to both the mystical and apostolic traditions. In the character of Jeremiah we can discover these links if we are willing to forego a more traditional understanding of prophets and prophecy.

The person whose life reflects the vocation of the prophetic office and way of life lived in the context of the prophetic tradition, and who, in turn, can thus be viewed as a "prophet," speaks about concrete things and events, hears the silent sigh of the powerless and oppressed, feels the pain of the oppressor, and intercedes to God for all. Gifted with tremendous passion, heightened sensibilities, and enlivened imagination, the prophet speaks with authority the hard word that wells up and gushes forth from the deep reservoir of uncompromised love. Often living life both on the periphery and on the cutting edge, the prophet is someone who remains faithful to God, faithful to the community, and faithful to the mission, even if it means having to stand alone. A servant of the divine word and vision, the prophet becomes the one capable of leading all to wholeness and holiness in the measure that the prophet is willing "to act justly, love tenderly, and walk humbly with God" (Mic 6:8). Jeremiah, the central actor in the book of Jeremiah, is God's prophet and the living symbol of God's fidelity to a community even in its most depraved state and painful moments. In Jeremiah, Israel can find hope. In the midst of destruction and Exile, he lives on in his words. He is God's promise to Israel that, indeed, the final word is not death but life. The drama of Jeremiah's life unfolds in a series of events that finds him confronting not only the political and religious leaders of his day but also his own people as well as the leaders and peoples of other nations. Through his proclamations and those people with whom her interfaces in the course of his mission and ministry we are able to catch a glimpse of his character that continues to challenge, inspire, and disturb people today who encounter him amid the leaves of the biblical text.

Jeremiah: Preacher of Grace, Poet of Truth

The book of Jeremiah opens with a superscription that contextualizes Jeremiah historically (1:1-3). Immediately following the superscription, Jeremiah the character introduces himself to us. He begins his life story by sharing with us who he is. His understanding of himself and his life's work was not something he arrived at on his own. It was revealed to him by God, and this divine revelation is the first word Jeremiah shares with us. Jeremiah tells us that God had chosen him to be a prophet before he was born, and that, despite his reluctance, he really had no choice in the matter. He was going wherever and to whomever God would send him, and as far as his feelings of inadequacy were concerned, they were not to be stumbling blocks. God knew what Jeremiah needed. God prepared Jeremiah's mouth for speech, provided him with the necessary words, made him a promise of enduring divine presence and deliverance, and gave him knowledge of his mission. This mission involved the destruction of an old world order and its myriad injustices and experiences of exile. The new world order that would emerge gradually from the ashes of the old would be characterized by justice, covenant relationship with God, and right relationship with one another.

As he narrates his life story, Jeremiah tells us that as part of his vocation as a prophet he was the recipient of intuitive visions, some of which included a branch of an almond tree (1:11), a boiling pot (1:13), and good and bad figs (24:1-10). Each of these visions was connected to divine revelations about what was to befall his people and his land because of the people's wicked ways. He also tells us that his life as a prophet entailed a series of divine promises meant to strengthen him internally so that he could deliver the divine word of judgment against the whole land—against the kings of Judah, its princes, its priests, and all the people of the land. Jeremiah tells us that God promised to make him a fortified city, an iron pillar, and a bronze wall (1:18-19). His strength would not be his own; it would be a divine gift.

Jeremiah also tells us that as part of his prophetic work he had to perform various symbolic actions like remaining celibate (16:1-4) and buying a field during the siege of his people's land (32:1-15).[10] These symbolic actions served not only to offer his people a warning of the disasters about to befall them, but also to give them a promise of hope that they could remember when disaster struck. Restoration, not destruction, annihilation, or exile, was God's ultimate intention and vision.

---

[10] For other examples see Jer 13:1-11: the linen loincloth; 13:12-14: the wine-jars; 19:1-15: the broken earthenware jug; 25:15-29: the cup of God's wrath; and 27:1-22: the sign of the yoke.

Jeremiah's proclamations provide us with an insight into his multi-faceted work as a prophet. The content of his proclamations also sheds light on his character. With candor, boldness, and searing honesty, Jeremiah railed against the prophets of his day—those who are false prophets (5:13, 30-31; 14:15-17; 23:9-40) and those who, as true prophets, have corrupted their prophetic office and vocation (23:13-15). He exposed the hypocrisy of the priests (5:31; 27:16-22) and the foolhardiness of other religious leaders (10:21), and he did not cower before kings (22:11-30; 27:1-15; 34:1-22; 37:1-21) or people in general whose injustices he tried to stop from becoming a permanent part of the fabric of daily life (5:20-31; 6:13-15; 9:1-6; 10:1-16; 17:1-13). His confrontations uncovered not only the hard-heartedness of his people but also their arrogance. They were without the capacity to be critically self-reflective, and consequently they saw themselves as "innocent" (2:35). They rested in their thought that God had turned divine anger away from them (2:35) because in their eyes they had not sinned (2:35).

Such hard-heartedness evoked two responses from God. Jeremiah tells us that, on the one hand, God is completely anguished over the wicked state of the people (4:9-31). Jeremiah communicates God's word, experience, and grief: "My joy is gone; grief is upon me; my heart is sick" (8:18, 19-21; see also 4:19-31). On the other hand, Jeremiah lets us know that God is completely disgusted with the people's wrongdoings and covenant betrayal (11:17). Jeremiah tells us how God ordered him not to pray for the people (7:16-20; 14:11-12). God's disgust and anger, however, are not the prevailing sentiments. Jeremiah reminds us that he repeatedly called the people to return (3:14), to repent (3:14; 4:1-4), to take up weeping and wailing (9:10). Further-more, Jeremiah assures the people that God will not be angry forever, if only the people will acknowledge their guilt (3:22-23). The people, however, did not repent; they refused to return to God (8:4-13). Jeremiah has given us a view into the hardened nature of his people and has shown us through his proclamations how disconnected they are from their God and God's ways (5:1-3). Despite the people's hard-heartedness and God's grief and anger, God, as Jeremiah tells us, will remain faithful to covenant relationship. Healing after divine chastisement and restoration after exile are promises that, in time, will come to fulfillment (23:1-8; 30–31; 33:1-13). Thus we see that Jeremiah's vocation as a prophet is bittersweet, and even if the divine word to be proclaimed is either bitter or sweet, Jeremiah makes no distinction in his efforts. He simply proclaims it even though it may cause him pain and distress at times (11:18-20). He performs his task faithfully. He lives out his vocation as prophet regardless of its cost to him personally, though he shows us that he is not silent about his struggles, nor is he shy in expressing his sentiments to his God (20:7-18).

The main character with whom Jeremiah interfaces throughout his life is God, who gives Jeremiah the word that must be proclaimed, who shows Jeremiah what the future holds for his land, his people, and his world, and who compels Jeremiah to address all sorts of people. Jeremiah has shown us not only the hard-heartedness of his people but also, as depicted by the biblical writer, the retributive side to God who threatens to bring evil upon peoples and nations for the evils they have done (11:17). Jeremiah is aware of this retributive side of God and appeals to it. Jeremiah wants divine retribution on his enemies (11:18-20; 12:1-4; 18:19-23; 20:12). God's response, however, is neither retributive nor compassionate. God, instead, challenges Jeremiah to remain steadfast in his ways (12:5-6). Despite all odds, Jeremiah trusts in his God (20:11), hopes in his God (20:13), and in the face of divine sovereignty and power he does not flinch from expressing his strong feelings about God to God directly (10:25; 15:15-18). He even challenges God about God's ways (5:3). Jeremiah, God's prophet whom God has empowered, is not shy and retiring in his relationship with his God. He is assertive. Just as God calls Jeremiah to task, so Jeremiah calls God to task.

As Jeremiah's relationship with his God continues to unfold in the midst of his unfolding life story, we see an unassuming side to Jeremiah's life. He did not immediately realize that some of his own people were indeed his "enemies," plotting against him (11:18-19). He became aware of his fate, as well as the people's evil deeds, only after God made such things known to him (11:18). He also had to rely on God to help him distinguish between true and false prophets (14:13-18). Thus Jeremiah learns what he has to know in the course of his life and mission as a prophet. Both his strength of character and his knowledge and awareness evolve in relation to his vocation, until he is able to say to the officials and people in his land: "But as for me, here I am in your hands. Do with me as seems good and right to you" (26:14). Having grown confident in God's promise to deliver him, Jeremiah continues to be faithful to his God and his mission, and when he encounters persecution (20:1-6) and life-threatening experiences (38:1-6) he neither fights against nor curses his enemies. His non-aggressive response remains constant and sheds light on his inner strength, his faith, his single-heartedness and single-mindedness, and his commitment to justice and the divine vision and hope for transformation. Even though he takes no action against his enemies except to talk to them directly, he remains true to himself and does speak out in justice on his own behalf (37:13-14). He is quick to confront King Zedekiah about the unjust imprisonment the king imposed on him (37:18-21).

Jeremiah's interfacing with other characters shows us not only his strength of character but also his strong sense of self. Under divine compulsion to proclaim God's word, he remains self-possessed with regard to his own experiences suffered on behalf of the divine mission given to him. He expresses his agony to his God, but to his enemies he raises a question that points up their wickedness (37:18), offers a word of encouragement after acknowledging God's role in his work and in their lives (26:12-13), and simply endures his unjust persecution, which becomes the impetus for one person—Ebedmelech the Ethiopian and "outsider"—to speak to King Zedekiah on Jeremiah's behalf. Ebedmelech acknowledges the injustice done to "the prophet Jeremiah" by the men who acted "wickedly" in throwing him into a cistern to die (38:8-9). Little did Ebedmelech know, perhaps, that the king had washed his hands earlier of Jeremiah's fate when he handed the prophet over to the officials who told the king lies about Jeremiah's activities, claiming that he was seeking the people's harm and not their welfare (38:4-5). The intercession of one righteous man, Ebedmelech, saves Jeremiah's life (38:10-13) and gives us an insight into God's saving activity, which is accomplished not only directly by God, but also through people.

Finally, Jeremiah, God's prophet par excellence, is a great poet skilled and trained in the rhetoric of his day. He has the capacity to engage an audience, as evidenced by his people's responsive reactions to him. A man of symbolic action, Jeremiah is a maker of metaphors and a weaver of images. Through the use of various literary techniques he captures with gusto the realities of both his day and his community, and despite his having to make harsh and disturbing announcements he tells his audience the truth about themselves, their life with their God, and the perceived threat about to befall them. Thus even Jeremiah's most foreboding messages are moments of grace, if only his people will heed his word and respond accordingly. It is my view, then, that both the judgment and salvation proclamations offer a double-visioned sense of hope, one that demands a change of heart and could lead to redemption, and one that bespeaks restoration and renewal, leading to transformation. Jeremiah's great love of God and God's people, his firm commitment to a divinely ordained sense of mission, his willingness to be God's servant-leader, so much so that his life is profoundly knitted to God and God to him, his rhetorical skill as an orator, and his openness to bear the cost of being prophetic, no matter what it may be, make him a preacher of grace and a poet of truth.

What follows in the next chapters of this book is a glimpse of Jeremiah interfacing with the most important person in his life—God—who in turn pushes Jeremiah to "interface" with the people of his day. All these characters with whom Jeremiah interfaces show us that God's vision for salvation and transformation is accomplished through relationship and the interaction with the events of daily life, both locally and globally.

CHAPTER ONE

"Now the Word of the LORD Came to Me . . .":
A Poet Graced, A Prophet Afflicted

Introduction

Little did Jeremiah realize that when God extended the divine hand to touch his mouth, his life would never be the same. Known by God before he was formed in the womb, consecrated and appointed a prophet to the nations before he was born, and destined to become a "fortified city, an iron pillar, and a bronze wall against the whole land" (Jer 1:18), this person named Jeremiah, who saw himself as "only a boy" (Jer 1:6), had no idea what was in store for him. He had no idea that for many he would become a poet graced as he himself became a prophet afflicted. This first chapter begins the magnificent story of a marvelous biblical character who, as God's prophet, is a reminder of God's enduring, transformative presence and compassionate face even when all is lost and seems for naught. As God's prophet this man called "Jeremiah" is a thorn in his people's side, but at the same time he is their greatest hope. And so begins the poetic story of a prophet and the journey of his life.

Jeremiah 1:4-10: Call and Commission

For Jeremiah the drama of his life begins with his divine call and commission (1:4-10), a vocation given and a directive revealed that will eventually turn his own personal world upside down and inside out as the physical world around him spirals downward toward its own demise. And yet, there is hope. . . .

Following a brief superscription that situates Jeremiah and his message in a historical context, Jeremiah addresses his unnamed and thus timeless audience with a familiar statement: "Now the word of the LORD came to me"

(v. 4). Immediately Jeremiah engages his audience with his straightforward-ness and story-like proclamation signaled by the word "now," which he uses in a narrative rather than a temporal sense. One can picture Jeremiah enthu-siastic and filled with a sense of awe and wonder from having had an ex-perience of God and having been encountered by God's word, an experience he just cannot wait to share with others. From a historical and narrative perspective verse 4 gives authority to Jeremiah's proclamation and helps to legitimate him as a prophet.

In verses 5-10 Jeremiah recounts his wonder-filled experience, which involves a dialogue between God and Jeremiah. God tells Jeremiah:

> "Before I formed you in the womb I knew you,
>> and before you were born I consecrated you;
> I appointed you a prophet to the nations."

By using a poetic catalogue of verb clusters—"I formed you," "I knew you," "I consecrated you," "I appointed you"—Jeremiah emphasizes that his voca-tion is divinely ordained. Furthermore, by twice repeating the word "before," Jeremiah forms a unity of time and sense between the first and second colon, and indicates to his audience that it was indeed God's intention that he should be a prophet. "I formed you" recalls the creation account (cf. Gen 2:7), "I knew you" implies intimate knowledge, and "I consecrated you" connotes being "set apart." Through the use of the phrase "I appointed you a prophet to the nations" Jeremiah lets his audience know the extent of his mission.

Jeremiah next shares with his audience his candid response to God:

> "Ah, Lord God! Truly I do not know how to speak,
>> for I am only a boy."

Jeremiah reveals to his listeners and readers his initial hesitation and unease at such a mission. His comments indicate how he perceives himself: unskilled and without the wisdom needed for such a daunting task. Jeremiah then acknowledges that God was not going to accept his lack of skill and wisdom as an excuse. His next words, "But the Lord said to me," continue to frame and unify the dialogue. Jack R. Lundbom notes that "this introductory phrase, which is repeated in verses 9, 12, 14; 3:6 (expanded), 11; 11:6, 9, and else-where, is precisely the phrase that introduces the 'prophet like Moses' prom-ise of Deuteronomy 18:17."[1] On a rhetorical level the use of this phrase at this point in the book of Jeremiah situates Jeremiah in the prophetic tradition of Moses.

---

[1] Jack R. Lundbom, *Jeremiah 1–20*. AB 21A (New York: Doubleday, 1999) 233.

In verses 7-8 Jeremiah again quotes for his audience what God had said to him:

> "Do not say, 'I am only a boy';
>> for you shall go to all to whom I send you,
>> and you shall speak whatever I command you,
> Do not be afraid of them,
>> for I am with you to deliver you,"
>>>>> says the LORD.

Here Jeremiah makes known to his listeners and readers God's rebuttal of his argument, and also points out that his mission will be divinely directed and lived out within the context of divine promise. With this divine promise given, God ushers Jeremiah into the company of renowned ancestors who have also received the same promise: Jacob (Gen 28:15), Moses (Exod 3:12), Joshua (Josh 1:5), Gideon (Judg 6:16), and others. This same promise will be repeated to Jeremiah two more times (see 1:19 and 15:20), and will also be extended to Israel (30:11). With this divine promise Jeremiah foreshadows his own personal experience (see Jeremiah 38–39), which will one day be Israel's, after the people's experience of exile. This promise later becomes a source of hope for Jeremiah in the context of his painful suffering (Jer 20:11-13).

Jeremiah next recounts God's further interactions with him (vv. 9-10). God touches Jeremiah's mouth, and in so doing gives him the divine words he needs to accomplish his mission. This action on God's part fulfills what was promised in Deuteronomy 18:18; Jeremiah is a "prophet like Moses."

Jeremiah then relates the last part of his story. After God had put the divine words into his mouth, Jeremiah learned the full extent of his task:

> "See, today I appoint you over nations and over kingdoms,
> to pluck up and to pull down,
>> to destroy and to overthrow,
>> to build and to plant."

What Jeremiah learns is that God's intention for him in verse 5 has now become part of God's commissioning him (v. 10). Jeremiah's verb clusters indicate the types of activities his vocation will entail. In the context of the book of Jeremiah and its overall message the verbs speak of both judgment and hope. Embedded in these verb clusters are royal and agrarian images that apply to both foreign nations and Israel. Lands will be ravaged, monarchies toppled, cities and a temple destroyed, but only to pave the way for new building and new planting in a new world order. Devastation, then, will not be for the sake of annihilation, but rather for the purpose of reconstruction, rebuilding, restoration, and renewal—a new life lived in accordance with God's ways and vision.

Looking at the passage as a whole, listeners and readers experience Jeremiah not only as a marvelous poet but also as a great storyteller. Like Moses, Jeremiah talks with God as one would with a friend. The dialogue indicates a level of trust and intimacy between God and Jeremiah. God has entrusted Jeremiah with a vocation and mission and, though reluctant at first, he embraces God's desire, call, commission, and mission. For Jeremiah's listeners and readers this passage establishes the prophet's credibility and authority as a prophet. For Jeremiah's own people the message for them is that in their midst is one who is empowered by God and will act with God's power. Such a person is both a source of hope and a figure to be feared.

From Jeremiah's poetic story of his experience with God we also receive an understanding of God and God's intentions. Jeremiah's God is one who plans to remain interactive in human lives and in the course of history, who has a divine plan of salvation in whose unfolding humanity plays an intricate role. Jeremiah's God is persuasive, caring, reassuring, and yet determined.

Finally, Jeremiah's poetic story makes clear that a direct encounter with God is possible for humanity. The contents of that encounter, when revealed, become prophetic insofar as they reveal something about the mystery of God and God's ways.

Jeremiah 1:11-19: Revelation, Challenges, and Promises

Having told his listeners about how he was called and commissioned by God (Jer 1:4-10), Jeremiah continues his story by describing his further encounter with God and the two visions that were part of that experience. The phrase "the word of the LORD came to me . . ." subdivides verses 11-16 into two smaller units, 11-12 and 13-16. In the first subunit the main symbol is an almond tree branch; in the second it is a boiling pot. Both symbols are related to the impending doom that is about to befall the southern kingdom, Judah: the Babylonian invasion that will result in the loss of land, the burning of the Holy City Jerusalem, and the devastation of the Temple. Furthermore, in both subunits there is a natural exchange of dialogue between God and Jeremiah. This encounter and exchange provide credence to Jeremiah as a prophet and situate him in the context of the entire prophetic tradition. He has had an experience of God, the contents of which are meant to inform and serve as a warning to his own community.

To look at verses 11-16 more closely is to discover something about the characters of God and Jeremiah through their interaction with each other. We can also, perhaps, come to a better understanding of what an experience of God is like in the context of the prophetic tradition. In this passage Jeremiah is not only telling his audience a story; he is also teaching them a lesson. Let's listen:

> The word of the LORD came to me, saying, "Jeremiah, what do you see?" and I said, "I see a branch of an almond tree." Then the LORD said to me, "You have seen well, for I am watching over my word to perform it." The word of the LORD came to me a second time, saying, "What do you see?" And I said, "I see a boiling pot, tilted away from the north."
>
> Then the LORD said to me: Out of the north disaster shall break out on all the inhabitants of the land. For now I am calling all the tribes of the kingdoms of the north, says the LORD; and they shall come and all of them shall set their thrones at the entrance of the gates of Jerusalem, against all its surrounding walls and against all the cities of Judah. And I will utter my judgments against them, for all their wickedness in forsaking me; they have made offerings to other gods, and worshiped the works of their own hands. But you, gird up your loins; stand up and tell them everything that I command you. Do not break down before them, or I will break you before them. And I for my part have made you today a fortified city, an iron pillar, and a bronze wall, against the whole land—against the kings of Judah, its princes, its priests, and the people of the land. They will fight against you; but they shall not prevail against you, for I am with you, says the LORD, to deliver you. (vv. 11-16)

When Jeremiah says to his audience, "The word of the LORD came to me," he is sending them a double message. First, he wants his listeners to know that what he is about to tell them is not something he concocted. Rather, it is a word that "came" to him. Hence it is a message that seems to have been revealed to him intuitively at first, which he later preached, and which was later written down. Second, Jeremiah wants his listeners to know that the origin of the message is divine: God is its initiator (vv. 11, 13). For Jeremiah's listeners this simple phrase is meant to lend authority and credence to his two visions and the messages they contain for his community.

The fact that God calls Jeremiah by his first name before saying anything else to him indicates that Jeremiah is known by God (see 1:5). The dialogue that ensues between God and Jeremiah both in verses 11-12 and in verses 13-16 reveals a certain level of intimacy between God and Jeremiah. God speaks to Jeremiah as one would with a friend; God asks him two simple questions and Jeremiah responds in kind. God's questions and Jeremiah's responses indicate a certain sense of mutuality in the relationship. Jeremiah's ability to see the symbols God has placed before him, coupled with God's affirmation that Jeremiah has "seen well" (v. 12), confirms that Jeremiah understands God's message.

With a sense of intimacy established, and a knowledge base affirmed, God entrusts still more to Jeremiah. God reveals to him the divine intention and plan that are prepared for the people of Judah. The revelation Jeremiah receives, which he must tell to his people, is ominous. Beyond even this, God allows Jeremiah to become privy to God's plan for him, a plan that carries with it an implied promise of mutuality but this time is more hierarchical in tone and less friendly: "Do not break down before them, or I will break you" (v. 17). In verses 14-19 one can detect a shift in tone. Here God sounds more like an instructor teaching and informing Jeremiah in a more discursive, less intuitive way than in verses 11-13. For Jeremiah, however, one fact remains clear: he has been instructed by God and entrusted with God's mission—"But you, gird up your loins; stand up and tell them everything that I command you" (v. 17a). He now lives under divine threat (v. 17b) and divine promise (vv. 18-19).

When Jeremiah delivers his message to his community members they learn that: (1) his message to them comes from a credible source (but whether or not they believe its content remains questionable); (2) their holy city, Jerusalem, and Judah are going to be invaded and taken over by the Babylonians, an event that originates with and is sanctioned by God, who is "watching over" the divine word to perform it; (3) they themselves stand guilty before God, judged and condemned for having fallen out of right relationship with God by violating the covenant when they forsook God, made offerings to other gods, and then worshiped the works of their own hands; (4) Jeremiah is now different from them; he has been set apart by God (vv. 17-19) and is guaranteed God's presence and divine deliverance insofar as he remains faithful to God's mission and commands.

The original community who heard Jeremiah's message was probably enraged by his words. Their transgressions have been exposed publicly through Jeremiah's proclamation of his encounter with God, and they now know where they stand with God: judged and condemned. What a chill must have run up their spines when they heard of the impending invasion! As for Jeremiah, he has now become an enemy to the corrupt among his own people. He is no longer one of their comrades. Instead, he belongs to the God they have forsaken, and if they have turned away from God, Jeremiah can rest assured that they will now turn against him.

Audiences today who listen to or read Jeremiah 1:11-19 learn several additional lessons about God, Jeremiah, and what we could call an experience of the divine in the context of the prophetic tradition. We can say at least six things about how God appears in this passage. First, Jeremiah shows us that God can be very personal, capable of interacting with human beings. Second, when God wants someone to learn something, God as teacher uses both inductive and deductive methods. Ordinary and common elements from life and, in Jeremiah's case, elements from his natural world and those common to his life experience are used in such a way that they become symbols of something greater than meets the ordinary eye. In the prophetic tradition symbols and symbolic actions become revelatory of the human and the divine; they help to communicate what is yet to unfold. Third, Jeremiah's posture as someone being instructed by God offers an insight into how God can communicate knowledge, namely, through the use of our intuition and imagination. Fourth, while the proclamation of God's word is an auditory experience full of rhetorical and historical inferences and references, the actual encounter with God is a deeply personal experience that can involve our internal sensibilities, and in turn can affect our auditory and visual perceptions of reality. Fifth, within the context of the prophetic tradition Jeremiah's experience makes clear that an encounter with the divine is not meant to be of a self-serving nature or purpose, for the human person is engaged in the encounter. The encounter with God often carries with it knowledge for and about something related to a person's community and informs that person of his or her role and mission within the context of the community and world. An encounter with God assures all life of God's enduring presence in the midst of creation and the course of history as it unfolds. Finally, Jeremiah's experience of God makes clear that God will not tolerate infidelity. There will be consequences.

The proclamations of Jeremiah reveal many aspects of his inner character. First, he is perceptive and intuitive and very capable of responding to God's questions. Second, he is gifted and graced by God—he has been entrusted with a direct experience of God, one of "hearing," with visual images serving the purpose of instruction. Third, although Jeremiah's life is prophetic by virtue of his creation, when God's *ruach* ("spirit") was breathed into him he did not choose to be God's prophet; he was appointed and consecrated by God before birth (1:5), given a divinely-ordained mission that required specific tasks, and then gradually strengthened and transformed by God so that he could fulfill the divine tasks and mission. Fourth, empowered by God, Jeremiah is "under" God's power. Last, Jeremiah's message about and portrayal of God reflect the theology and culture of the prophet's day. On the one hand God is depicted as friendly and personable; on the other hand God is the one "in control" and "watching over" the divine word in order to fulfill it. Jeremiah's God is portrayed as a tit-for-tat God who will bring disaster on the Judahites because of their infidelity. Jeremiah's reading of his times and the inevitable takeover by the Babylonians is interpreted through his own theological lenses, which seem to be colored by the deuteronomistic theology of retribution (see Deuteronomy 28).

In summary, chapter 1 of the book of Jeremiah sets the stage for the entire development of Jeremiah as a character and the book as a whole. What will be seen in subsequent pages of this study is how Jeremiah evolves into God's prophet as a preacher of grace and a poet of truth in the context of his mission (v. 10), and how the foreshadowed transformation of Jeremiah from a boy (v. 6) into a "fortified city," "an iron pillar," and "a bronze wall" against the whole land takes place, along with the unfolding of the divine promise: "I am with you, says the LORD, to deliver you" (v. 19). Last, in looking at verses 4-10 in relation to verses 11-19 one observes two literary styles: poetry and prose. What makes these verses prophetic, and for that matter the book as a whole, is the dynamic relationship that exists between the characters of God and Jeremiah, revealing the direct and purposeful intervention of God into the life of Jeremiah and Jeremiah's disclosure of the entire experience and its contents in a way that is both poetic and prosaic. Jeremiah the person and preacher, together with his craft as a poet and a storyteller, have become the means and the medium by which revelation occurs.

Jeremiah 2:1–3:10: A Divine Indictment

Jeremiah 2:1–3:10 is a series of oracles that have been woven together into a coherent narrative whose theme is Israel's and Judah's sinfulness and God's powerful condemnation and indictment against the people as a whole. Although this passage is composed of several small poems, its overall structure is made up of two literary units: a proclamation of remembrance (2:1-3) and a judgment proclamation (2:4–3:10). Throughout the entire passage Jeremiah stands center stage, proclaiming God's message to his listeners. What Jeremiah was called and commissioned to do in 1:4-19 he now does, beginning with a focus on the house of Jacob (2:4–3:5). Thus the drama of Jeremiah's life as a prophet commences as the beginnings of a coherent narrative start to take shape on a literary level.

A Proclamation of Remembrance (2:1-3)

Jeremiah's mission begins in 2:1-3. No longer being told *about* his mission, he is being commanded to carry it out. God tells Jeremiah to go and proclaim the divine word that has been revealed to him, and Jeremiah does as he is commanded:

The word of the LORD came to me, saying: Go and proclaim in the hearing of Jerusalem, Thus says the LORD:

> I remember the devotion of your youth,
>> your love as a bride,
> how you followed me in the wilderness,
>> in a land not sown.
> Israel was holy to the LORD,
>> the first fruits of his harvest.
> All who ate of it were held guilty;
>> disaster came upon them,
>>>>>> says the LORD. (2:1-3)

The phrase "the word of the LORD came to me saying" (v. 1) recalls 1:4, 11, 13 and thus links Jeremiah's call and commission to his mission: we see him living out his call and going forth as commissioned. Jeremiah is the poetic preacher of the message, but God is the one who speaks through the prophet. Lundbom succinctly outlines the rhetorical function of verses 2b-3 in the context of the book of Jeremiah as a whole:

> As lead oracle, 2:2b-3 introduces the entire apostasy-repentance col-
> lection of 2:1–4:4. . . . The present oracle has an even broader func-
> tion, i.e., to introduce both the apostasy-repentance collection (2:1–4:4)
> and the foe-lament collection (4:5–10:25). Verse 2b is a foil for the
> oracles on apostasy, and v. 3 for the oracles on the foe from the north.
> In the Jeremiah book we see evidence of an "outbuilding" process.[2]

In this proclamation Jeremiah depicts God remembering the goodness, the holiness of Israel in its youth. He captures God's sentiments through the use of two metaphors: Israel as a bride (v. 2), and Israel as the "first fruits" of God's harvest (v. 3). All who treated Israel unjustly or came after Israel received their "just deserts" in return. This suggests some sort of divine judgment against Israel's enemies resulting in a punitive retribution that, according to the deuteronomistic theology of retribution, could be interpreted as coming from the hand of God. With the reference to the "wilderness" Jeremiah appeals to the exodus tradition and the trust Israel had in God early in their covenant relationship. This also recalls Hosea's preaching, when God promised to bring Israel into the wilderness to speak tenderly to Israel's heart (Hos 2:14-15). In the days of Hosea, too, Israel had gone astray (see

---

[2] Ibid. 251.

Hos 2:1-13). Jeremiah's use of the past tense is telling: "Israel was holy to the LORD" (v. 3).

By casting God's speech in the form of a remembrance proclamation, and by comparing Israel to a bride and the first fruits of God's harvest, Jeremiah calls his audience to think back on their past when Israel's love was young, devoted, and trusting, to recall the covenant relationship that existed between God and Israel, and to be mindful that the land belongs to God (see Lev 25:23), with Israel as the first fruits—first fruits that also belong to God (see Exod 23:19) and are God's harvest as well. By sandwiching the phrase "Israel was holy to the LORD" (v. 3) between the two metaphors Jeremiah sets up a contrast by way of implication. Without casting any judgment on Israel, Jeremiah lets Israel know that it is no longer holy. In not condemning Israel outright, Jeremiah works to capture the attention of his audience by appealing to the memory of the community's past lived experience. Once he has their attention he can lower the boom, which is what happens in Jer 2:4–3:5. Thus verses 2b-3 set the stage for Jeremiah's next proclamation.

In summary, Jer 2:1-3 portrays Jeremiah as a prophet, once again entrusted by God with God's word. It also shows Jeremiah being faithful to God and God's ways. Jeremiah's rhetorical devices and strategy show him to be a skilled and savvy orator who knows how to preach to his primary audience. Jeremiah's message also sheds light on God and the relationship that exists between God and Israel. In verse 2a God talks to Israel very personally, as signaled by the use of first- and second-person pronouns. In verse 3, however, beginning with the phrase "Israel was holy to the LORD," the tone becomes more impersonal as God talks about God's self and Israel in the third person. This shift in tone mirrors the shift in relationship between Israel and God. They have grown distant from each other on account of Israel's present state, which is "unholy" to the LORD. Heard from the perspective of God, Jeremiah's message becomes a song of lament. The interface that occurs between God and Jeremiah, with Jeremiah delivering God's message, testifies to the unity that exists between God and the prophet as they work together to carry out the divine mission.

Readers and hearers of today will be impressed by the intimate relationship that exists between God and the prophet. The text sheds light on the character of Jeremiah, but also reveals the love relationship that existed between God and Israel in ancient times, a love relationship that was not only metaphorically marital but also intrinsically hierarchical and patriarchal. Israel "follows" God in the wilderness, and as first fruits Israel is to be understood as belonging to God. Furthermore, Israel's God was a God of power who could use that power punitively to another's detriment, as implied by the last verse of the text. Thus the character of God as portrayed by Jeremiah reflects both the culture and the theology of an ancient world.

Jeremiah's Judgment Proclamation (2:4–3:10)

Having set the stage with his first proclamation (Jer 2:1-3), Jeremiah now delivers his second (2:4–3:5), and again he focuses on Israel: "Hear the word of the LORD, O house of Jacob, and all the families of the house of Israel. Thus says the LORD . . ." (2:4).[3] Jeremiah does not always invite his audience to listen; he commands them to hear the word of the LORD and speaks with ultimate authority: "Thus says the LORD." Jeremiah's own strong and clear voice has prepared the ears of his listeners for an even stronger voice they will now hear—God's voice—delivering a blunt, shocking, "knock your socks off" message. A people once holy to the LORD has become estranged from its God, its partner in covenant. God with righteous anger confronts them, and through Jeremiah's voice gives expression to the felt anger, pain, and indignation that many within the community have caused because of their violation of covenant and consequent estrangement from God and God's ways. Let us listen now to God's message that Jeremiah the poet-preacher delivers.

JEREMIAH 2:4-13

Jeremiah casts the first part of God's message (Jer 2:4-9) into the form of a "classic indictment, asserting that Israel has forfeited the relationship with YHWH."[4] Jeremiah begins this "classic indictment" with God's recollection of Israel's past, thus inviting the listeners of his community to enter into reflection and remembrance as well. This spirit of recollection and remembrance continues the tone and sentiment of Jer 2:2-3. In verse 5a Jeremiah uses a rhetorical question to begin God's personal recollection:

> What wrong did your ancestors find in me
> > that they went far from me,
> and went after worthless things,
> > and became worthless themselves?

---

[3] Lundbom notes that the superscription in 2:4 "points to a Northern Israel audience, which could be exiles in Assyria, or those living in the old territory of the Northern Kingdom, or both" (ibid. 258). With respect to the historical background of Jer 2:4-9 in particular Lundbom suggests that this proclamation was probably "one of Jeremiah's earliest, and a date soon after 622 B.C. is as good a proposal as any." He observes further that the spirit of reform (rather than outright judgment) fits well; in this spirit people were offered the opportunity to repent, "and . . . Jeremiah, in this and the prior oracle, brings to the people a message entirely consonant with views formulated at the highest levels of government" (ibid. 263).

[4] Walter Brueggemann, *A Commentary on Jeremiah: Exile and Homecoming* (Grand Rapids: Eerdmans, 1998) 34.

Expecting no reply to this rhetorical question, and keeping his audience focused on their ancestry, Jeremiah continues:

> They did not say, "Where is the LORD
>   who brought us up from the land of Egypt,
> who led us in the wilderness,
>   in a land of deserts and pits,
> in a land of drought and deep darkness,
>   in a land that no one passes through,
>   where no one lives?"

Jeremiah's clever use of rhetoric and rhetorical devices continues to keep his audience not only silent, but also ensconced with God in the memory of past experiences as he, Jeremiah, brings forth the next part of God's message:

> I brought you into a plentiful land
>   to eat its fruits and its good things.
> But when you entered you defiled my land,
>   and made my heritage an abomination.
> The priests did not say, "Where is the LORD?"
> Those who handle the law did not know me;
>   the rulers transgressed against me;
>   the prophets prophesied by Baal,
>   and went after things that do not profit. (2:7-8)

By assuming God's voice ever so personally, Jeremiah focuses his audience's attention on God, who now zooms in on Israel's ancestors. No longer talking about them with Jeremiah's audience listening in, God now talks to them directly and recalls all the personal divine effort and goodness that were bestowed on them: "I brought *you* into a plentiful land. . . ." God also makes the Israelite ancestors remember what they had done in spite of all the divine favor bestowed on them: "But when you entered you defiled my land . . ." (v. 7b). Continuing in this same spirit of recollection, God then recalls for the ancestors how the religious and political leadership among them had gone astray and become prey to corruption. The sin of Israel's ancestors was apostasy and idolatry. Jeremiah, recalling it in the presence of the listeners of his day, reminds his community of the past and makes them aware of their family's sins that ultimately led to the downfall of the Northern Kingdom, Israel. The punch line to the whole unit comes in verse 9:

Therefore once more I accuse you
    says the LORD,
and I accuse your children's children.

Wham! Having accused Israel's ancestors in the past for their infidelity and wicked deeds, and having exposed their infidelity and transgressions in the hearing of Jeremiah's listeners, God once again accuses Israel's ancestors of infidelity and transgression, even though these ancestors have died. The second part of God's accusation now comes into focus: "and I accuse your children's children" (v. 9b). Not only have the ancestors been accused, but also their children's children, specifically Jeremiah's addressees—the house of Jacob and all the families of the house of Israel. With a subtle progression of interlocking thoughts and an appeal to a common Old Testament retribution formula,[5] Jeremiah has taken his audience by surprise. He has disclosed their infidelity and transgression with grace and style. He has paved the way for the next part of his message; above all, he has been faithful to his divine mission.

Jeremiah continues to shed light on his audience's infidelity and transgressions in a manner that directly "exposes" their wickedness. In verses 10-13, the second part of Jeremiah's long proclamation, God is the main speaker, addressing two imaginary audiences: (1) messengers God has dispatched to the Greek islands and to Kedar, and (2) the heavens. Verse 10 features a series of imperatives: "cross . . . look . . . send . . . examine . . . see." Here Jeremiah creates for his listeners an image of God gathering information via messengers. The rhetorical question in verse 11 clarifies the mission of the messengers:

Has a nation changed its gods,
    even though they are no gods?

The focus on other nations' fidelity to their gods makes an indirect statement about Israel's God and monotheism. The rhetorical question invites the answer, "No," which in turn results in another indirect condemnation of Israel:

But my people have changed their glory
    for something that does not profit. (v. 11b)

---

[5] See, e.g., Exod 20:5; 34:7.

Both God and Jeremiah, by their word and message, have once more un-covered Israel's waywardness and delivered it to them in their ear. Having heard this statement, along with the rhetorical question just before it, Israel has now been made aware by Jeremiah of its grave offenses, warranting cosmic condemnation.

By means of triple imperatives and an apostrophe Jeremiah communi-cates God's dismay at Israel's deeds, and lets the people know that God has called on the heavens to act against them:

> Be appalled, O heavens, at this,
>> be shocked, be utterly desolate,
>>> says the LORD. (v. 12)

With this third command God orders the heavens to withhold rain, which would cause a drought, dry up the land, and bring famine upon the people. Jeremiah has now provided his audience with a prospect of impending events. Walter Brueggemann notes:

> It is no wonder that the great cosmic powers, heaven and earth, observe this sorry situation and are stunned (Jer 2:12). Heaven and earth in this poem (cf. Isa 1:2) function as witnesses who guarantee oaths and ob-serve patterns of faithfulness and fickleness. Because heaven and earth know Yahweh to be the true God (cf. Ps 96:11), Israel's shabby response to Yahweh is exposed for what it is. In this cosmic court there is no doubt about the guilty party.[6]

And why should the heavens be appalled, shocked, and utterly desolate at Israel's "changing its glory for something that does not profit"? With candid-ness and metaphorical language, the poet presents God's case further:

> for my people have committed two evils:
>> they have forsaken me,
> the fountain of living water,
>> and dug out cisterns for themselves,
> cracked cisterns
>> that can hold no water. (v. 13)

Essentially the two evils are but one: Israel has abandoned God for other gods. By metaphorically describing God as the fountain of living water

---

[6] Brueggemann, *Exile and Homecoming,* 36.

Jeremiah depicts God as a fertility god. Israel has cut itself off from the source of life. The nation of Israel digging out cracked cisterns for itself is symbolic. Lundbom unpacks Jeremiah's image of the cistern:

> These are holes dug into the foundation to collect water when spring water is unavailable or to store water from some natural water supply. Cistern walls were plastered to make them watertight, but the plaster could crack, in which case the water would become unusable or would seep into the ground. Broken cisterns were therefore useless.[7]

Thus Israel has rejected God, the fountain of living water, and has put its trust in leaky cisterns that are unusable for holding water. Jeremiah's use of metaphor and symbolism communicates a single thought to his audience: Israel has cut itself off from life. Embedded in the broken cisterns is the allusion to the Baals, which are generally associated with fertility. No rain from the heavens (v. 12), out of relationship with the fountain of living water (v. 13b), and in possession of broken cisterns (v. 13c)—Israel's fate is sealed. The people are doomed to die. What a harrowing message Jeremiah has just delivered to his audience! What Jeremiah has made clear is that Israel, once holy to the Lord and the first fruits of God's harvest (v. 3), has chosen its own fate.

JEREMIAH 2:14-19

In the next section of Jeremiah's message to Israel there is an allusion to an earlier poem (2:1-3). The unit opens with Jeremiah commenting on Israel, raising two interrelated rhetorical questions that point up Israel's identity as understood by God (v. 14a). Both questions expect "no" as a response. "No," Israel is not a slave; Israel has been called to be God's "servant" in the best sense of the term (Jer 30:10; Isa 42:1). And "no," Israel is not a "homeborn servant," which would imply that Israel was born in its master's house and thus considered a slave from birth. Israel was chosen by God because God loved Israel, redeemed by God from the house of slavery, joined to God through covenant, and entrusted by God with God's holy law (see Deut 7:7-11). With these two rhetorical questions Jeremiah invites his audience to remember who they are and to hear God's utter bewilderment at them, expressed more directly through a third question: "Why then has he become plunder?" (v. 14b). This is what God thinks about Israel, namely

[7] See Lundbom, *Jeremiah 1–20,* 268.

that in light of who Israel is, none of what has happened to it or will happen to it has been within the divine plan. The use of the present perfect tense, known in Hebrew grammar as the "prophetic perfect," signals what has already happened to Israel historically and what is about to happen. The prophetic perfect tense is also known as the tense of vision. Jeremiah makes his audience see their past history through God's eyes and tries to make them see what their future holds in a way that makes it seem that the future has already happened. The prophetic perfect tense carries with it the sense of certitude. Hence Israel's past and future is going to be the same: devastation. All these points are made clear through the imagery in verses 15-16.

Jeremiah's metaphors present God replaying Israel's past and foreshadowing its future (vv. 15-16). The "lions" (v. 15) refer to the Assyrians.[8] With their infiltration and takeover of the Northern Kingdom, Israel was laid waste and its cities left in ruins, without inhabitants. Many of the Israelites had been either killed in battle or deported by the Assyrians. By using the plural "lions" Jeremiah opens up the possibility of another interpretation of the metaphor. In the historical context of this passage the "lions" are also the Babylonians, the most powerful empire in the world and Judah's enemy to the North whom God will raise up against Judah on account of Judah's transgressions (see Jer 1:15). Thus, embedded in the images of Israel's destruction and the metaphor of the lion is Judah's future fate, made clear in verse 16. Here Jeremiah adds another dimension to the metaphor and imagery already begun:

> Moreover, the people of Memphis and Tahpanhes
> have broken the crown of your head.

This image is an allusion to the Egyptians, who will eventually turn on Judah as well. The crown that has been broken hints at Jerusalem's fate. The question to be asked is: Do Jeremiah's listeners understand thus far the warning he has given them through the message he has delivered, the scenes he has recalled, and the pictures he has created?

In verses 17-19 Jeremiah, in the voice of God, speaks directly to his listeners and drives home the point that everything that has befallen Israel in the past and all that will befall the Israelites and Judahites in the future is the result of the people's own doing the moment they forsook God and broke

---

[8] Contra Lundbom (*Jeremiah 1–20*, 271–72), who sees the lions as representing only the Babylonians and Egyptians. He does not see the "lions" of former times, the Assyrians, being alluded to in this text.

the covenant relationship. Implied in this text is the deuteronomistic theology of retribution (see Deut 28). The people's wickedness and apostasies will be the source and cause of God's retribution and punitive justice.

JEREMIAH 2:20-22

In verses 20-21 Jeremiah's thought pattern and rhetoric present his audience with two implied contrasts that on the one hand highlight God's goodness in the face of Israel's depravity (vv. 20-21a), and on the other hand show up Israel's uncleanness despite its attempt at washing (v. 22). To accent his first contrast he uses two metaphors. Depraved Israel has become like a whore, even though God planted it as a choice vine from the purest stock. The harlotry image is associated with Baal worship, and the vine image recalls Isaiah 5. Both are related to fertility, with Baal being the god of fertility and Israel's God often assuming that *persona* as creator and LORD of creation. The rhetorical question Jeremiah voices on behalf of God is self-explanatory and harks back to verse 17. Israel is in its degenerate state because of its own choice, beginning with its forsaking God. Jeremiah makes sure his audience realizes that God has not forgotten Israel's guilt. What remains a mystery, though, is whether Israel—and Judah in Israel's mirror—truly sees itself and hears Jeremiah's and God's word. If God's people have abandoned God, how can they even begin to understand Jeremiah, the one sent by God? Still, Jeremiah's voice and God's presence among the community remain persistent and constant, a sign of hope and a testament of God's enduring love and fidelity to covenant.

JEREMIAH 2:23-29

With metaphor upon metaphor, complemented by rhetorical questions and quotes within quotes, Jeremiah gives voice to God's indignation over Israel and Judah while setting the stage for his blistering indictment yet to come (see Jer 2:35).

Jeremiah, continuing to assume God's voice, opens this segment of his message with a rhetorical question that once again points at the people's apostasy. The two metaphors that follow, namely "a restive young camel interlacing its tracks" (v. 23c) and "a wild ass at home in the wilderness, in her heat sniffing the wind" (v. 24a) symbolize the people's "lustful behavior."[9]

---

[9] Ibid. 282.

In verse 25b Jeremiah quotes God quoting the people:

> But you said, "It is hopeless,
>> for I have loved strangers,
>> and after them I will go."

Through this rhetorical device Jeremiah points up the people's resolve not to change their ways. They see themselves as too far gone. By articulating the people's statement back to them, however, Jeremiah allows them to hear themselves, and in so doing he hopes, perhaps, that after hearing their own pitiful state and attitude they might reach out for help. This may not be the case with God, though, who after quoting the people next lays out for them in metaphorical language the shame that is to come upon them because of their decision not to reverse their course:

> As a thief is shamed when caught,
>> so the house of Israel shall be shamed. (v. 26a)

The parade of indictments—"they, their kings, their officials, their priests, and their prophets"—indicates that both the people and their leadership will be shamed because they are all depraved, as revealed by their own words that God quotes (v. 27a).

In verse 27b, when Jeremiah again quotes God, he draws attention to the root of the people's problem:

> For they have turned their backs to me,
>> and not their faces.

This people turn to God only when they are in need. God offers them a stinging rhetorical response that points up their foolhardiness:

> But where are your gods
>> that you made for yourself?
> Let them come, if they can save you,
>> in your time of trouble;
> for you have as many gods
>> as you have towns, O Judah. (v. 28)

The final vocative adds an element of surprise. Not only is Israel guilty of apostasy, but also Judah! The rhetorical question in verse 29a, followed by

God's comment in verse 29b, pulls together the thought of verses 23-29. Here Jeremiah sheds light on God's righteousness and indicts both Israel and Judah: "You have all rebelled against me, says the LORD."

JEREMIAH 2:30-37; 3:1-10

The people's final upbraiding occurs in verses 30-37, with the climax in the last three verses. The words are still the words of God. In verse 30a they describe some of the pain of God's past relationship with Israel:

> In vain I have struck down your children;
> > they accepted no correction.

This God who is madly in love with the people is someone who has exerted punitive chastisement over them in their times of waywardness. To Jeremiah's listeners this comment would be frightening. If former generations have felt the blow of God's hand as a corrective measure, then why should this wayward generation think it will be any different for them if they do/do not acknowledge their transgression and guilt, repent and return to God? The deuteronomistic theology of retribution that underlies the prophetic texts, that has shaped the prophet's and people's theology and their idea of God, leaves the audience of this text bewildered, perhaps, and contemporary audiences in a quandary as to how to understand and make sense of an Old Testament God who is shown to feel justified in exerting violence as a means to an end.

After several more expressions of divine rage over the people's behavior, including their pretense of innocence (v. 35a), Jeremiah delivers God's final decision:

> Now I am bringing you to judgment
> > for saying, "I have not sinned." (v. 35b)

Jeremiah's entire message thus far, with all its metaphors, rhetorical questions, symbols, images, and quoted speeches has led up to this point. God's people stand accused and indicted, Israel first and then Judah (see Jer 2:8). The extended metaphor in 3:1-5 harks back to 2:2. Israel, the one who loved God so much in the early days of the marriage, has become another man's wife. Israel, God's chosen one, has forsaken God and chosen the Baals. And Judah, Israel's younger sister, did not learn from having seen and heard about her older sister's experience (see Jer 3:6-10), but rather has followed in her sister's ways, without returning to God (3:10).

Jeremiah 2:4–3:10 in Context

By delivering this incredibly graphic message to Israel and in Judah's hearing as well (see 2:2, 28), Jeremiah has set the stage for his mission—"to pluck up and to pull down, to destroy and to overthrow" (1:10)—a mission that will continue to unfold throughout his lifetime and throughout the book as whole. One can imagine how incensed Jeremiah's audience became on hearing one of their own people proclaim such a message with the declared authority of and often in the very voice of God. It is no wonder that this poet will become a man repulsive to and rejected by his own, who lie in wait to put an end to him.

Jeremiah 2:4–3:10 also provides many insights into the character of Jeremiah and what type of person the historical Jeremiah might have been. First, Jeremiah as a character is wedded to his God and to God's mission. He proclaims what God tells him to make known and often assumes God's voice while doing so. Second, Jeremiah is committed to shoring up and renewing the loving relationship that once existed between God and God's people. One way of helping the people find their way back to God is by identifying the root cause of why the relationship has gone sour, exposing that root cause, helping the people see it, and then working persistently to get them to change their choices and course to the point of estrangement. Jeremiah's work as a preacher demonstrates that he is taking the steps necessary to try and bring his people back to their God. Third, as a preacher Jeremiah is not only a gifted orator but also a poet. His words reveal his genius for putting together a speech that is highly imaginative, well-crafted, and candid so as to appeal to his audience's intellectual, emotional, psychological, imaginative, and religious sensibilities. Fourth, as a prophet Jeremiah carries out with power and strength that dimension of his vocation that challenges him to call people to holiness. His message portrays his persistent efforts at this task. Often transparent in his person, Jeremiah as a character provides his audience with an insight into who God might be and what are God's ways. But because everything is historically, socially, culturally, and religiously conditioned, both the prophet and God, along with God's ways as revealed by the biblical text, must be held up for ongoing critical theological reflection, and appropriated and understood accordingly. What is clear about Jeremiah as a prophet from his words thus far is that his mission is divinely ordained and brings with it the authority, power, prowess, freshness, creativity, candidness, boldness, strength, energy, and persistence characteristic of the Spirit of God. Jeremiah is someone who "cuts to the chase," one on whom God's favor rests.

Jeremiah 3:11–4:4: Return, O Faithless Children

Besides exposing a people's breach in covenant relationship with God, a prophet also has the responsibility of helping that people find their way back to God. The words of Torah, "Be holy, for I am holy" (Lev 11:44-45) ring in the prophet's ear and become a driving force for the divinely entrusted mission. Although God can become fiercely and justly angry at the Israelites who seemingly have fallen out of love and right relationship with the One whose heart had been set on them from the beginning (see Deut 7:8), this God of faithful and steadfast love (Exod 34:6) never stops reaching out to those who have gone astray and have become estranged. The prophet cannot give up on the people, either. Jeremiah 3:11–4:4 is a wonderful story set to poetry that Jeremiah proclaims, revealing the desire of God's heart.

Looking at 3:11–4:4 as a literary whole, we can detect several rhetorical subunits:

3:11-12a	Superscription: Statement about faithless Israel and false Judah
3:12b-14	Address to Israel and Judah
	vv. 12b-13 Plea to faithless Israel
	v. 14 Pleas to faithless children: Israel, with Judah implied
3:15-18	Divine promise and vision of restoration: A united house
3:19-25	A divine reflection: A liturgy of repentance
	vv. 19-20 Statement to Israel
	vv. 21-25 Statement to the faithless children: Israel, with Judah implied
4:1-4	Address to Israel and Judah
	vv. 1-2 Conditional statement
	vv. 3-4 Exhortation and threat

Within and among these units and subunits are various rhetorical elements that reveal Jeremiah the character as a poet of great genius. These rhetorical elements help to unify the poem, whose interlocking units contribute to the poem's overarching theme: return, repentance, restoration.

Jeremiah 3:11 sets the stage for the entire passage, which will focus on Israel and Judah (3:12-14, 15-18, 19-25; 4:1-4). In the first main unit (3:12b-14) the phrases "Return, faithless Israel" (v. 12b) and "Return, O faithless children" (v. 14) link the two subunits together. The reference to Zion at the end of the unit (v. 14) leads into the next unit (3:15-18), where Jeremiah speaks about Jerusalem (v. 17). Zion/Jerusalem represents the whole nation. The reference to the house of Judah and the house of Israel at the end of this second unit (see v. 18) leads into the third unit (3:19-25), where Jeremiah addresses Israel and Judah. The pastoral imagery in verse 15 and verse 24, coupled with a reference to the "ancestors" in verses 18, 24, and 25 also adds to the coherence between the two units. Finally, 3:19-25 is joined to 4:1-4, the last unit, through common addressees: both units focus on Israel and Judah, with the idea of Israel returning to God linking this last unit to the first one (4:1; 3:12).

Collectively, all the units are addressed to Israel and Judah, and all develop the themes of "return" and "repentance" with the exception of 3:15-18, which speaks of "restoration": God to the people, the people to God, and Israel and Judah to each other. Then there will be one God, one people, and one kingdom, with Jerusalem as God's throne—God's holy city—the center of the united kingdom, to which all nations shall come and be transformed (v. 17). If 3:15-18 is seen as the heart of the entire literary unit (3:11–4:4), one could say that Jeremiah uses his rhetorical skill to make a powerful theological statement: restoration to and transformation into God by God is contingent on a people's return to God—to right relationship—through their repentance of the ways that caused their state of estrangement in the first place. Simultaneously, a return to God (3:11, 14) with acknowledgment of one's guilt (3:13) is the way to restoration and unity (3:17-18), a divine promise offered and one that leads to the transformation of others. Jerusalem, then, becomes the main symbol on which this whole Jeremiah passage turns. Ironically, Jerusalem is where Jeremiah delivers his most profound message (see Jeremiah 7 and 26).

Jeremiah 3:11-12a

Jeremiah begins his speech with a raw comparison: "Faithless Israel has shown herself less guilty than false Judah" (v. 11). Jeremiah is now privy to what God thinks about Israel and Judah, and by announcing it he makes his audience privy to God's thoughts as well. The Israelites and Judahites hearing Jeremiah have just learned how God sees them, and the Judahites have been informed that God sees them as worse than the Israelites. They would also perhaps see Jeremiah as someone standing apart from them and acting in a way that smacks of self-righteousness. After all, he is a community member pointing the finger at his own. From a rhetorical perspective this verse is ironic. On the one hand Jeremiah's comment condemns the entire community; they are all either faithless or false—a rotten bushel of apples. On the other hand there is one among them who is part of the bushel but not in the basket with them—Jeremiah himself, who is the embodiment of fidelity and truth. In any case, verse 11 is an indictment of Israel and Judah. By using the word "then" at the beginning of this verse that opens 3:11–4:4 Jeremiah signals to his audience that there is and was a sense of progression to this encounter with and experience of God, and he also adds a sense of narrative unity to his poetic proclamation.

In verse 12a Jeremiah makes clear to his audience that God is the one who directed him to make the proclamation that follows in 3:12b–4:4. From a rhetorical perspective, Lundbom notes that "the designation of an audience in 'the north' intends to make clear that 'Rebel Israel' is Northern Israel, even though in verse 18 both Israel and Judah are said to be returning 'from the land of the North.'" From a historical perspective Lundbom goes on to say that "'the north' could be the place of exile in Assyria (2 Kgs 17:6) or else the old Northern Kingdom, where many original inhabitants still live."[10] Because the text is obscure, it is possible for multiple audiences to be hearing Jeremiah's word.[11]

Jeremiah 3:12b-14

Jeremiah directs his opening lines to Israel (vv. 12b-13). Verse 14 is addressed to Israel as well, but now with Judah implied. Giving utterance to God's voice, he pleads with Israel to return to God and to acknowledge its guilt, and then spells out for the people once again what they are guilty of. This elaboration is another divine indictment, but this time it is done indirectly and in the context of a sincere call to return (vv. 12b-13). A second call to return is given in verse 14. Jeremiah's metaphorical vocative, "O faithless children," now draws Judah into the picture, with the rest of the verse focused on a promised return to Zion. In this verse God makes no bones about the relationship with Israel and Judah: "I am your master."

The Israelites and Judahites listening to Jeremiah receive a clear picture of where they stand with God and where God stands with them. God sees them as "faithless," and although they have written God off, God has not written them off. Even though they have heard and experienced God's anger in the past, God promises to be merciful to them as well. But there is one thing they must do, and that is to acknowledge their guilt and transgression.

---

[10] Ibid.; see also Herbert G. May, "The Ten Lost Tribes," *BA* 6 (1943) 58; and David C. Greenwood, "On the Jewish Hope for a Restored Northern Kingdom," *ZAW* 88 (1976) 381.

[11] Lundbom, *Jeremiah 1–20,* 311, where he suggests that the audience might be "people in Judah, exiles in Egypt, Babylon and Assyria, and those living in the old territory of Northern Israel." Lundbom proposes a date of 597 B.C.E. or later for the material.

Thus God is willing to meet the people halfway if they will meet their God halfway.

From what God communicates about God's self to and through Jeremiah, Jeremiah's past and contemporary audiences learn several lessons: (1) that God does get angry over infidelity and that such anger is justifiable and righteous; therefore human anger over infidelity is also appropriate, justifiable, and righteous; (2) that God's gaze upon a transgression is also one of mercy—compassion—and not one of anger, and by extension, judgment; (3) that God's feelings of anger can pass if the guilty party acknowledges his or her offense; (4) that God's ultimate plan is for unity (see vv. 14 and 18); and (5) that the relationship between God and the people is hierarchical, with God as the "master."

For contemporary audiences, too, the lessons gleaned from the text can be challenging because they call people to "be holy" as God is holy. This would suggest embracing a way of life characterized by fidelity, compassion, and justice that acknowledges one's own pain and the injustices of another that may have caused such pain. Acknowledgment of this sort by both parties or more would allow personal and communal integrity to flourish.

Jeremiah 3:15-18

In this next section Jeremiah offers his audience a word of hope and a magnificent vision of long-awaited restoration and unity. God wants nothing more than to be reestablished with the people, but in a new and different way:

> I will give you shepherds after my own heart, who will feed you with knowledge and understanding. And when you have multiplied and increased in the land, in those days, says the LORD, they shall no longer say, "The ark of the covenant of the LORD." It shall not come to mind, or be remembered, or missed; nor shall another one be made. At that time Jerusalem shall be called the throne of the LORD, and all nations shall gather to it, to the presence of the LORD in Jerusalem, and they shall no longer stubbornly follow their own evil will. In those days the house of Judah shall join the house of Israel, and together they shall come from the land of the north to the land that I gave your ancestors for a heritage. (vv. 15-18)

Once restored to their God, the people will one day be restored to their land as well. Jerusalem will be reestablished and expanded, and even the Gentiles will come to it. God's city will be a home for all the peoples of the earth (cf. Isa 2:1-4; Mic 4:1-5). Jeremiah's temporal references, "at that time"

(v. 17) and "in those days" (v. 18) indicate the eschatological nature of the message. Both the prophet and God have given the people a word of hope and a vision yet to unfold. Historically, Jeremiah lived to see Jerusalem destroyed, and although he experienced the end of the southern kingdom and the Temple as well, this message given to him by his God was not only a source of hope for his people but also the probable seed of light he carved in his own heart in his bleakest hours (cf. Jer 20:13; 31:31-34, 38-40; 32:26-44).

Jeremiah 3:19-25

This rhetorical unit consists of two parts: God's lament song (vv. 19-22) and the Israelites' and Judahites' lament song (vv. 23-25). In vv. 19-20 Jeremiah expresses God's dashed hopes and dreams for the people—plans for giving this people the best land and hopes for a most intimate relationship with them as their "Father," a relationship characterized by unswerving fidelity. But this did not happen; Jeremiah's metaphor of the faithless wife captures Israel's relationship to God (cf. 3:11, 14, 22).

Through family imagery and a marital metaphor Jeremiah has not only communicated to his audience God's sentiments, but has tried to show them what they have lost through infidelity, probably has tried to make them feel guilty by letting them hear God's sadness, and above all has indicted them again for their apostasy. Here we need to recognize that Jeremiah's imagery is culturally conditioned and the metaphor is gender-specific. Israel is pictured as a child, with God represented as a male deity and head over the family, and thus the image is both patriarchal and hierarchical (cf. 3:14). Furthermore, the metaphor of Israel as God's wife could color our religious imagination negatively. Because this metaphor is historically, culturally, and religiously tied to covenant, with God understood as "husband," the metaphor can only fit one gender—the female—which feeds into an older understanding of Eve as the first human to cause estrangement from God. Thus Jeremiah's rhetoric needs to interface with contemporary thought and audiences if the biblical text is to remain a living tradition, with the prophetic imagination offering new metaphors to help transform age-old attitudes and problems.

In verses 21-22 Jeremiah portrays God imagining the faithless people lamenting and, as God states why Israel's children are weeping, the people stand indicted once again by the prophet and by God. Finally there comes a poignant word from God and a promise:

> Return, O faithless children,
> I will heal your faithlessness.

Israel and Judah have received an invitation and God continues to imagine the words of their "plaintive weeping" (vv. 22b-25). In God's imagination Israel and Judah have acknowledged their offense.

Jeremiah 4:1-4

The tone of the passage shifts in 4:1-4, yet the same divine plea is heard. This time it is couched in a series of conditional "if" clauses that Jeremiah uses to reinforce in the people's hearing that God's graciousness is contingent on their actions. In these verses one can hear the ever-so-slight echo of 3:12b-13. Finally, in verses 3-4 God, through the prophet, addresses Judah directly. The messenger formula authenticates Jeremiah as a credible prophet and lends divine authority to his forthcoming proclamation. The agricultural imagery of 4:3b is an allusion to Hos 10:12 and indicates what Israel must do to escape God's anger and judgment. In the command given to the Israelites to circumcise themselves to the LORD and to remove the foreskin of their hearts, Jeremiah appeals to Torah (Deut 10:16). For the ancient people both Torah and the prophets were associated with revelation. By appealing to the tradition and by stacking four imperatives together Jeremiah sends the Judahites a strong message with rhetorical grace: heed God's advice or else prepare to endure the consequence (v. 4b). Finally, by the image of circumcising the foreskin of one's heart Jeremiah reminds his audience that covenant involves more than outward signs; it is "an affair of the heart" (see Deut 7:7).

In sum, like a solitary drummer Jeremiah beats out the same message over and over again with rhetoric and semantic variations on a theme. True to his God and his mission, his words reveal the marvelous relationship he shares with God and the great love God has for the people. With God he exposes what is and envisions what can be. And though steeped in the theology and culture of his day, which colors his imagination and consequently his rhetoric, Jeremiah remains constant in his cause and persistent in his preaching, reminding his audience that in spite of their weakness, fickleness, and infidelity there is still hope.

In Retrospect

Selected texts studied in this chapter have provided an initial introduction to and insight into the complex person of the character Jeremiah, beginning with his call and commission as a prophet and continuing through his early preaching. Charged with the mission to proclaim God's word, and entrusted with that word, Jeremiah is seen as one faithful to his task, but with no apparent support from his community. Their own voices are not heard except where they are quoted by God through Jeremiah; these quotations reveal (1) their stubborn and recalcitrant attitude toward God: "I will not serve" (Jer 2:20); (2) their inability to acknowledge their infidelity to God and covenant: "I am not defiled, I have not gone after the Baals" (Jer 2:23), "I am innocent; surely his anger has turned away from me" (Jer 2:35a), and "I have not sinned" (Jer 3:35b); (3) their own sense of personal desperation when they do achieve some self-realization: "It is hopeless, for I have loved strangers, and after them I will go" (Jer 2:25); (4) their own misguided understanding of themselves: "who say to a tree, 'You are my father' . . . and to a stone, 'You gave me birth'" (Jer 2:27a); and (5) their ultimate dependence on God when crisis strikes: "Come and save us!" (Jer 2:27c). To this community Jeremiah offers a word of truth. His proclamations keep exposing their sinful ways to them while expressing God's anger at them for their infidelity to covenant and to their love-relationship with their God. And yet, to this stubborn, recalcitrant, wayward people who see themselves and their situation as "hopeless," Jeremiah holds out a graced word. He lets them hear God's dashed hopes and dreams, God's anger and frustration, but above all he lets them hear the desire of God's heart: "Return . . . I will not look on you in anger, for I am merciful . . ." (Jer 3:12c) and God's divine intent: "In those days . . ." (see Jer 3:15-18).

As a skilled orator with a highly developed rhetorical style, Jeremiah makes transparent the dynamic relationship that exists between the human and the divine. And because his message is both timebound and timeless he offers audiences today the opportunity to enter into critical theological reflection to understand the contours and continuity of the prophetic word and its tradition as it continues to unfold in text and life. Both Jeremiah the character and Jeremiah the book are still but deep waters, waiting to reveal the next "pearl of great price."

CHAPTER TWO

"Declare This in the House of Jacob . . .":
A Portrait of Uncompromising Fidelity

Introduction

As we have seen, Jeremiah is a highly gifted and complex character, and his work within his community and among the nations is equally complex. In this chapter we will concentrate on Jeremiah's words of alarm, his words of consolation, and his new covenant, all of which provide us with an insight into the breadth of the prophet's mission. The rhetorical devices Jeremiah uses to communicate his message remind us of his skill as an orator.

A person with a broad mission, and called to be a prophet both to Israel and to the nations, Jeremiah is constantly on the move from person to person, place to place, proclaiming God's word and making known God's ways. He goes to the people in the streets, to the houses of kings, to a potter's house, and he even takes time to write in a book all the words God has spoken to him. His message of justice is disturbing. His words of hope are comforting. He stands in the midst of peoples and nations, persistently, patiently, and passionately calling them back to right relationship and to the embrace of fullness of life for all. A sign opposed, a person rejected, he faithfully does his work of plucking up and pulling down, destroying and overthrowing, building and planting by delivering God's creative word that strikes at the heart to chasten, to renew.

Words of Alarm

The short poem in Jer 4:5-8 shows Jeremiah being commanded by God to declare a message in Judah, in Jerusalem; as the book continues, Jeremiah is seen fulfilling God's command. He shouts out a divine word of doom and calls the people to mourn. Jeremiah's cry is a battle cry, signaled by the images of the trumpets and the standard. He is calling the people to prepare for war against a ferocious lion who is about to lay waste the land and its inhabitants. The lion, chief among all in the animal kingdom, is the symbol for the Babylonians, and Jeremiah's message foreshadows the Babylonian invasion of the Southern Kingdom of Judah and its demise. The twist in the poem occurs in verse 8:

> Because of this put on sackcloth,
>   lament and wail:
> "The fierce anger of the LORD
>   has not turned away from us."

The Babylonians, the enemy from the north, have been metaphorically summoned by God to invade the land as a means of divine chastisement for the people's apostasy, idolatry, and infidelity to covenant. Given the fact that the message is proclaimed in Jerusalem of Judah, Jeremiah's many listeners would most likely respond complacently because of their belief in the inviolability of the Holy City. Jeremiah's exhortation to mourn is a word of grace. If the people lament, then perhaps God's anger will be abated. This, however, is only a preliminary step forward. As will be seen in later texts, God desires not lamentation but rather a contrite heart that acknowledges one's transgression. We cannot tell from the text whether or not Jeremiah's primary audience understands his symbolism. One thing seems certain, however: he has caught their attention and has them wondering.

In chapter 13 Jeremiah is again commanded by God to speak a word to the people of Judah, and once again he obliges. In this brief prose narrative in the form of a judgment speech God outlines for Jeremiah exactly what he is to say and do and anticipates for him what his listeners' response will be. The central symbol of the narrative is a wine-jar. As the story unfolds, God commands Jeremiah to tell the people that every wine-jar is to be filled, a command to which the people will respond with a rhetorical question that points up their "knowing-ness": "Do you think we do not know that every wine-jar should be filled with wine?" (Jer 13:12).

God next tells Jeremiah to declare to the people that they will be filled with drunkenness and then be dashed against each other. God's final word that Jeremiah has to deliver is indeed harrowing: "I will not pity or spare or have compassion when I destroy them" (v. 14). Here the wine-jar symbolizes the people of Judah, and whether or not they make the connection is obscure from the text. One thing is clear: the people and their leaders stand indicted by God and are headed for an excruciating fate.

The narrative portrays Jeremiah carrying out his mission diligently, and although his message is foreboding, it does reveal to the people just where they stand with God, which affords them the opportunity to search out how they can avert such a fate. In this sense the prophet's message of doom is a grace-filled word. Knowing the truth about what is to befall them, the people could have a change of heart, acknowledge their transgression, return to God, and be saved from such an end. Do they, however, take the prophet and his word seriously? History records otherwise.

Jeremiah has more woeful words for the ears of his listeners. Another short poem in chapter 14, specifically verses 17-18, is a lament that God tells Jeremiah he must sing. It describes the horrors of war and its devastating consequences for the people and the land. The first part of the song is the lament proper: "Let my eyes run down with tears. . . ." The reason for the lament is that the people are struck down with a crushing blow, a grievous wound (v. 17). The poem's metaphorical language aims at engaging the people imaginatively.

The second part of the lament elaborates on the first part. The crushing blow and grievous wound are due to a military invasion and a famine. The element of irony is found in the poem's last line:

> For both prophet and priest ply
>   their trade throughout the land,
> and have no knowledge. (v. 18c)

Of all the people in the community, the prophet and the priest are supposed to be among the most knowledgeable. The prophet is inspired by God and the priest is well-versed in Torah. But what is it that they do not know?[1] God and Jeremiah leave the listeners in a quandary.

The lament is written as if these things had already happened, but in truth it foreshadows what is to befall the people—devastation from the invasion of the Babylonians. The crushing blow and grievous wound is a double entendre. On the one hand these are the results of war; on the other hand they come from what was thought to be God's punitive justice for the people's infidelity. The agents of God's punitive justice would be the Babylonians. With the hand of the deuteronomic editor and the deuteronomistic theology

---

[1] Peter C. Craigie, Page H. Kelley, and Joel F. Drinkard Jr. speculate what the prophet and priest do not know. "If they do not know the land, then the verse would refer to exile. If they have no knowledge and are wandering around in a daze, the verse could have in mind the results of invasion and defeat. The passage as a whole seems to picture a time after invasion but before the final deportation." (*Jeremiah 1–25*. WBC 26 [Dallas: Word Books, 1991] 203). While each of these possibilities is plausible, I suggest that what the prophet and priest lack is spiritual knowledge: they are unable to comprehend God's plan of action against a wayward people.

of retribution in the background, the text of Jeremiah suggests that in Jeremiah's day the Babylonians were conjured up by God as a way of chastising the people of Judah for their infidelity. Finally, what the prophet and priest do not know is what God is plotting to do—they are unable to perceive the ways of God. Jeremiah, however, can perceive God's ways, and he is given knowledge that he passes on to the people, only to have such knowledge counted as wind.

Jeremiah's word of judgment continues in chapter 18 in the narrative about a potter and clay. This story is a parable in two parts: verses 1-4 and 5-11. In the first part we see God instructing Jeremiah. The instruction involves a field trip to a potter's house. When Jeremiah arrives at his destination he observes a potter at the wheel, reworking spoiled clay into another design (vv. 1-4). Jeremiah makes no attempt to understand why he is having this experience; he waits on God for explanation, and sure enough, in the second part of the story God interprets Jeremiah's experience for him and reveals its significance. The text depicts God using a rhetorical question, a simile, and metaphorical language in general to enlighten Jeremiah on the meaning of his experience. The house of Israel is the pliable clay in God's hands that God will shape according to God's own desire, and according to the pliability of the clay. Significant in the passage is the point that what God intends to do with the clay is not always a hard and fast decision. God's mind is changeable; God works with the clay. Thus the fate of the house of Israel could be positive or negative, depending on how the people respond to God, just as the shape of the vessel depends on how clay responds to the kneading of the potter.

The last part of the parable contains a punch line: God will bring disaster upon Judah. Thus the first section of the second part addressed to the house of Israel serves as a lesson to Judah. In the last verse of the second part Judah stands indicted by God, because even though God has intended to build and plant Judah, Judah did evil in God's sight and will thus suffer consequences. But like the spoiled artwork in the potter's hand, Judah can be reworked; its fate is not absolute if the people turn, repent, and amend their ways.

God's word is creative and metaphorical, and Israel's God is a God who desperately wants to keep working with the people despite their spoiled condition. Jeremiah as God's prophet does and says what God asks of him; he is open to being instructed by God, and he delivers an imaginative word to his listeners. How the people respond is not known; that they have a choice is evident from the parable's content.

Jeremiah, as a prophet to the nations, speaks not only to the people of his own land but also to the people of foreign nations, beginning with Egypt.

The proclamation against Egypt is part of a larger and very rich tradition known as "the oracles against the nations." Gerald L. Keown, Pamela J. Scalise, and Thomas G. Smothers provide the social and historical framework for this proclamation:

> Oracles against foreign nations (OAN) appear in every prophetic book except Hosea. . . . The origin of the OAN tradition is to be found among the earliest practices of the Israelite people. The earliest of the OAN was the war oracle, summoning people to battle, pronouncing disaster for the enemy, and often including a taunt against the enemy. Characteristic of the war oracle was the imagery of the Lord (Yahweh) as divine warrior. . . . The concepts of Yahweh's universal sovereignty, of Yahweh's utilization of foreign powers to achieve divine purposes with reference to Israel, and of Yahweh's right to judge foreign nations existed at least as early as the eighth-century prophets. In the prophetic books, foreign nations are most often condemned for pride, military aggression, and idolatry. The OAN had three main purposes: (1) to pronounce doom on a foreign nation, sometimes for the mistreatment of Israel; (2) to serve as a salvation oracle or oracle of encouragement for Israel; (3) to warn Israel about depending on foreign alliances for their security.[2]

Jeremiah's proclamation against Egypt (in chapter 46) contains all the characteristics of a war oracle. It is part of a larger passage (Jer 46:1-26), the first twelve verses of which feature Jeremiah delivering a message of divine judgment against Egypt. The poem's setting is the battle at Carchemish in 605 B.C.E.[3] As a literary unit it functions as a taunt against Egypt and may also serve as a deterrent for those Judeans who seek an alliance with Egypt rather than submitting to Babylonian lordship. Verses 1-2 are introductory material, with verse 1 introducing the entire unit of proclamations against the nations (Jer 46–51). This verse connects the word of God to the foreign

---

[2] Gerald L. Keown, Pamela J. Scalise, and Thomas G. Smothers, *Jeremiah 26–52*. WBC 27 (Dallas: Word Books, 1995) 275.

[3] Verse 2 provides a detailed historical setting for the text, but Walter Brueggemann draws out the canonical-theological claim the verse asserts, which goes beyond the historical level. He notes: "the claim concerns the rule of Yahweh over the battle of Carchemish in 605 B.C.E., when Babylon emerged as a world power, thus jeopardizing Egyptian hegemony. This prose editorial comment appeals to the outcome of that battle as a reference point for Yahweh's governance amid world powers." (*A Commentary on Jeremiah: Exile and Homecoming* [Grand Rapids: Eerdmans, 1998]) 425.

nations' future, and leads to the development and fulfillment of Jeremiah's vocation as a prophet (see Jer 1:5).

Jeremiah opens the proclamation with a summons to war (vv. 3-4). God speaks the poem through the prophet. A string of successive imperatives, "prepare," "advance," "harness," "mount," "take your stations," "whet your lances," and "put on your coats of mail" creates a sense of urgency. Jeremiah does not, however, indicate who is preparing for battle. One can presume from v. 1 that the Egyptians are donning their armor. In verses 5-6 Jeremiah describes the warriors retreating. The rhetorical question posed by God in verse 5 indicates the warriors' panicked state. Essentially the fighters are powerless. But who is the mighty power overpowering the warriors? Verses 7-8 are a taunt. The question asked in verse 7 is answered in verse 8. The similes "like the Nile" and "like rivers," both used twice, add continuity and poetic rhythm to the poet's message. Together, verse 7 and 8a form a balanced chiastic structure. In verse 8b Jeremiah's personification lets the river speak, and here one learns that the river's aspirations are for disaster. Given the fact that Egypt is compared to the Nile, the likely conclusion is that like the Nile, Egypt too has dreadful aspirations. In verse 9 Jeremiah continues the call to action, rallying the horses, chariots, and warriors. What is the purpose of this preparation? Jeremiah gives no hints until verse 10:

> That day is the day of the Lord GOD of hosts,
>> a day of retribution,
>> to gain vindication from his foes.
> The sword shall devour and be sated,
>> and drink its fill of their blood.
> For the Lord GOD of hosts holds a sacrifice
>> in the land of the north by the river Euphrates.

The disclosure is shocking, the theology appalling. Warrior God is going to massacre Egypt. Here "the day of the LORD" is the day of judgment.

In verses 11-12 Jeremiah depicts God addressing Egypt directly. The blow about to strike Egypt will be lethal; there will be no healing. Egypt's shame will become public. Egypt will be as nothing in the sight of all the other nations.

In sum, Jeremiah bears a devastating word to Egypt. With rhetorical skill the poet leads his audience along until he unveils the whole picture in verse 10. Surely Jeremiah is now a prophet to the nations, and surely he must have been a reproach to the Egyptians. By delivering this message, however, he does afford them the opportunity to reform their ways. Those nations who have flaunted their power will now be brought low—they will be pulled down from their lofty pedestal by a God who is not only, according to the text, Lord of creation, God of Israel, but also Lord of the nations. This passage is inherently and overtly violent. It reflects the specific hierarchical and theological agenda that wants to make God sovereign over all. After the proclamation against Egypt, Jeremiah announces many more against the nations that are just as horrific as this one. Is this, however, the only message Jeremiah bears? Are judgment and doom the only words God gives him? The answer to this question rests between the pages of chapters 30–33, otherwise known as the Book of Comfort within the book of Jeremiah.

Words of Consolation

Perhaps one of the most beautiful passages in the entire book of Jeremiah is 31:1-26, the prophet's "dream." This passage is a series of proclamations centered around the theme of homecoming: God is bringing the exiles back home. In the midst of impending devastation and disaster, this passage offers a word and a vision of hope. The final prophecy will be compassion and restoration—"to build and to plant" (see Jer 1:10).

The proclamation of hope and restoration consists of several subunits: verses 1-6, 7-9, 10-14, 15-17, 18-20, 21-22, 23-25, and 26. Each of these subunits is distinguished one from the other either by a prophetic messenger formula or by a subtle shift in topic. The capstone of all the oracles is the opening verse: "At that time, says the LORD, I will be the God of all the families of Israel, and they shall be my people" (v. 1). By using the phrase "at that time" Jeremiah signals that this proclamation is eschatological. The main speaker of the entire passage is God, who speaks through the prophet Jeremiah.

Jeremiah begins his delivery of God's wonderful message in verse 2 with a striking vision of God as one who is, once again, madly in love with Israel. In verses 2-3 Jeremiah depicts God giving a profile of the exiles. They are a people who found "grace in the wilderness" and enjoyed an enduring and faithful relationship with their God. In verses 4-6 God speaks tenderly and directly to the exiles, declaring an everlasting divine love for them and promising them a return to a time of music and merriment as they once again plant vineyards in their homeland. The reference to the "mountains of Samaria" suggests that the original addressees of this proclamation were the remnant of the Northern Kingdom. God's quoting the sentinels, "Come, let us go up to Zion, to the LORD our God," foreshadows the rebuilding of the Holy City and the Temple.

The second proclamation (vv. 7-9) continues the sentiments of the first. Here God addresses an anonymous audience, asking them to rejoice over Jacob/Israel's good fortune. God outlines for the listeners the divine plan of regathering, reunion, and restoration. The final metaphor speaks again of God's bondedness to the people:

> . . . for I have become a father to Israel,
>   and Ephraim is my firstborn. (v. 9c)

In the third proclamation (vv. 10-14) God calls upon all the nations to listen to the jubilant message about to be revealed. The shepherd-sheep imagery Jeremiah uses to capture the relationship that now exists between God and Israel communicates a sense of care. The verbs "has ransomed" and "has redeemed," used in relation to Israel, speak of a theology of liberation. God is the one who sets free. The use of the prophetic perfect tense in present time indicates that what God is foreshadowing will indeed happen. The lush images of the grain, the wine, and the oil, together with the people's lives becoming "like a watered garden," all suggest fertility. The people and the land will be full of life, continually refreshed. This restoration will be an occasion for celebration as God promises to turn the people's mourning into joy, giving them comfort and gladness instead of sorrow. Thus, as the people turn to their God, so God turns to them and together they enjoy the fullness of life: ". . . and my people shall be satisfied with my bounty, says the LORD" (v. 14).

In the fourth proclamation (vv. 15-17) Jeremiah depicts God telling a brief story about Rachel weeping for her children (v. 15). In the next verse God addresses Rachel directly, offering her a word of comfort and assuring her that her children will come back to their own country. The end to Rachel's mourning will be the fulfillment of the prophecy delivered in Jeremiah 31:13.

In the fifth proclamation (vv. 18-20) Jeremiah portrays God assuring the identity of Ephraim in order to deliver Ephraim's confession (vv. 18-19). Here Ephraim is compared to an untrained calf who now pleads with God to take him back, especially after he has expressed repentance and contrition for his treacherous ways. The tone shifts in verse 20. Here God assumes God's own voice and identity to communicate God's true feelings toward Ephraim. The two rhetorical questions point up Ephraim's dearness to God, who "remembers" Ephraim even in the worst of times. To be "remembered" by God is to be blessed by God. God's final word to Ephraim is mercy.

Verses 21-22 are addressed to Israel, which is being called to journey back to God. The vocative, "O virgin Israel" offers an ironic image. God is calling apostate, idolatrous Israel "virgin." With repentance and restoration comes a new identity. God no longer sees Israel as it was; Israel is metaphorically returned to its chaste state before its time of infidelity (v. 21). The rhetorical question in verse 22 indicates that Israel is not yet fully restored to "right relationship," but God promises that in time it will happen. The image of the woman encompassing the man involves personifications of Israel and God. Adulterous Israel, divorced by God, now returns to embrace God once again (v. 22).

The last proclamation (vv. 23-25) speaks about the restoration of prayer. As the people are restored to the land, so shall they be returned to praise—the greatest form of prayer—and to one another. God's people now live under God's great care and promise of new and renewed life (vv. 24-25). But suddenly, in verse 26, Jeremiah awakes: the whole picture thus far was all a dream.

In summary, this multifaceted, multilayered proclamation features Jeremiah fulfilling another dimension of his prophetic vocation, namely, to be a herald of good news and a shining ray of hope. His wonderful message of return, restoration, and renewal to be accomplished through God's ever-lasting love and mercy sheds light on the divine plan, which is one of liberation, deliverance, salvation, restoration, and transformation. The Judahites exiled to Babylon and Egypt become a symbol of hope for all peoples, and while the gender-specific language metaphorically embedded in the text can be off-putting, readers and listeners today need to remember that the ancient tradition of covenant became associated with marital imagery in the time of the prophets, beginning with Hosea. Thus this text is also a reminder that new metaphors expressive of a community's religious experience are sorely needed.

A New Covenant

The most hopeful and tender passage in the book of Jeremiah is the one about the new covenant in Jeremiah 31:31-34. With poetic prose Jeremiah delivers God's word to the house of Israel and the house of Judah. This is a divine promise that speaks of a new relationship, one that will be initiated and sustained by God.

The promise opens with the phrase, "the days are surely coming, says the LORD. . . ." Although this promise is eschatological, it will happen. The covenant God will make will not be like the Sinai covenant that was written on tablets. It will be, instead, a covenant written on hearts. This law will be an attitude, a way of life that speaks of justice, righteousness, and lovingkindness. This new covenant will be mutual. Through love, all will know God, from the least to the greatest. For God's part, God promises to forgive the people's iniquity and forget their sins. The new covenant speaks of solidarity and union: a beacon of hope for sorrowing people.

In Retrospect . . .

The most striking quality of Jeremiah's life is his fidelity to his God and to the vocation and mission entrusted to him. As a prophet, he is called and commissioned by God to go to people and places where he perhaps would rather not go. He proclaims the divine word persistently. It is often a harsh and unwelcome word, and yet embedded in it is a grace, an opportunity for people to change if they choose. The first to confront his people, he is also the first to console them. His word of comfort, his message of hope, is a reminder for all times that God is a God of mercy and compassion who is perpetually about the work of liberation and transformation, of building and planting, of molding and shaping, of remolding and reshaping.

CHAPTER THREE

Gussied in Loincloth and Sporting a Yoke: Symbols Come to Life

Introduction

The texts studied thus far have shown Jeremiah to be a highly skilled poet, faithfully proclaiming God's word as designated by his divine calling and mission. Jeremiah, however, preaches in another way as well. Often without understanding why he acts in certain ways, Jeremiah performs various actions and makes certain choices that leave him wondering about such actions and choices. At other times he is commanded by God to perform various tasks of a symbolic nature, the understanding of which is sometimes given to him. Thus Jeremiah's life becomes the embodiment of the prophetic word he preaches. He becomes a living metaphor of God's ways—a symbol of the Divine, offering to audiences down through the ages a fuller sense of what being a prophet means within the prophetic tradition.

In the passages describing these symbolic actions[1] we see Jeremiah in his role as a storyteller, describing to his listeners, the people of Judah, how God had commanded him to perform a certain action and then revealed to him the significance of the action on behalf of Judah. In all of Jeremiah's stories we experience rhetoric as effective, persuasive communication.

Jeremiah 13:1-11: The Tale of a Linen Loincloth

This story of the linen loincloth is made up of two main parts (vv. 1-7 and vv. 8-11). It includes a triple divine command (vv. 1, 4, 6), a main symbol

---

[1] See Jer 16:1-4; 18:1-11; 19:1-2, 10-11; 27:1–28:17; 32:1-15; 43:8-13; 51:59-64.

—the linen loincloth—and an instruction (vv. 8-11). Jeremiah's symbolic act is a point of debate among scholars, and there is no conclusive evidence or suggestion from the text to say whether it might be a dream, a vision, a parable, or a symbolic action.[2]

Jeremiah opens his story, which he relates retrospectively, with a familiar messenger formula, but adding a personal touch: "Thus said the LORD *to me*" (v. 1). This phrase lends authority to what Jeremiah is about to say, signals to his listeners that his word is authoritative, and establishes the autobiographical nature of his comments. Jeremiah next describes what God commanded him to do, namely, to buy a linen loincloth, wear it, and refrain from dipping it into water (v. 1). Jeremiah does what God tells him to do without any question whatsoever (v. 2). Then he describes how the word of the LORD came to him a second time, with the command to go to the Euphrates River and hide the cloth there in the cleft of a rock, which he did (vv. 3-5). Finally, he tells his listeners what God said to him a third time, specifically, to dig up the loincloth, which by then had become "ruined" and was "good for nothing" (vv. 6-7).

In the telling of his story Jeremiah takes his listeners from one point to the next in a progressive manner that keeps them focused on him and his loincloth. He offers very few details and does not explain any of the symbols or gestures. Then, as if he were taking a blindfold off their eyes, he lets them "see" what God has in store for these Judahite listeners. For them and for Jeremiah's broader audience the point becomes clear: God is disgusted with the people of Judah because of their refusal to listen to God's word, their stubbornness in wanting to go their own way, and their egregious apostasy and violation of covenant (vv. 8-11). Central to this part of the story is Jeremiah telling the Judahites how God sees them: they are like the loincloth. Once a priestly people, they have now become nothing more than rotten, stinking, and dirty, no longer a part of God's "body" but separated from it, as distant from God as the Euphrates River is from Jerusalem.[3]

Whether or not Jeremiah grasped all the implications of his actions and the connections among all the symbols of his story is hard to determine.

---

[2] For further discussion see Robert P. Carroll, *Jeremiah*. OTL (Philadelphia: Westminster, 1986); Artur Weiser, *Das Buch des Propheten Jeremia*. ATD (Göttingen: Vandenhoeck & Ruprecht, 1969); Wilhelm Rudolph, *Jeremia*. HAT (Tübingen: J.C.B. Mohr [Paul Siebeck], 1968); John Bright, *Jeremiah*. AB 21 (Garden City, NY: Doubleday, 1965); Paul Volz, *Der Prophet Jeremia*. KAT (Leipzig: Deichert, 1928), among others.

[3] This image of the linen loincloth is most appropriate for the people of Judah. In ancient times priests wore linen loincloths (see Exod 28:39; 39:27-29; Lev 16:4; Ezek 44:17-18). Linen was the cloth of ordinary people as well (see, e.g., Judg 14:12-13; Prov 31:24).

Whether or not his primary audience fully understood the interconnectedness of the symbols is equally difficult to determine. One thing, however, is clear: all subsequent readers of the written story know plainly what God thinks of the Judahites and what will become of them.

Jeremiah's story sheds light on his character. Once again he is faithful to his mission. He delivers God's word, and this time the word is joined to him: he experiences it and then tells the story of his experience. There is also another element foreshadowed by his story: Jeremiah takes the loincloth off his body; it is no longer a part of him. Jeremiah is separated from the loincloth, separated from this sinful people, and the fate of destruction that overshadows his people will not be his fate. He may get dirty when he is thrown into the cistern and sinks into the mud (see Jer 38:1-6), but he is eventually rescued (Jer 38:7-13) and lives on long after Judah and Jerusalem are destroyed. Jeremiah is a further reminder that there will be a faithful remnant that will be saved from death. Finally, one also sees Jeremiah not only faithful in delivering God's word, but faithful to the word itself. When God speaks, Jeremiah responds.

Jeremiah's words also shed light on God as a character. This God who speaks to Jeremiah is a God forsaken by a people so loved and cherished and held so close. Thus forsaken, this God is angry and will deal with those who have walked out of the relationship to follow other gods. While Jeremiah's God is justified in feeling this way, certain theological questions need to be raised by today's readers and hearers of this story. What kind of God, the creator of all, calls a people "evil"? Are the people evil, or their intentions and deeds? What kind of God makes a people "cling" close so that they can be for God "a name," "a praise," and "a glory"? Is God's overwhelming care and love selfless, or does God love so that through his people other nations will come and pay homage to the "LORD of LORDS"? At best, Jeremiah's words and story betray a God whose depiction is culturally, historically, and theologically conditioned by social content of the storyteller's day. One would ask further, were all the Judahites unfaithful, or is one hearing a corporate view of the community that is accepted to the detriment of those who are faithful and guiltless?

Finally, God's words shed light on Jeremiah's community. Many of the people are profaned and stand judged by their God because of their apostasy, idolatry, and injustices done to one another. One can see why this people, living under the threat of divine chastisement, might not want to return to God. If only they could remember the tales of their ancestors, how they built a golden calf, how Moses smashed the tablets on that calf, how Moses then interceded for that people, and how God renewed the covenant . . . if only Jeremiah's people could remember. . . .

Jeremiah 16:1-13: The Symbolism of a Life of Celibacy

With all that Jeremiah has to do and bear for the sake of his fidelity to God, God's word, and God's mission entrusted to him, one would imagine that after many long hours on the road he would at some point return home to enjoy the comfort of a wife and family. But no, God had other plans for Jeremiah! The prophet's own personal saga continues as he remains faithful to all that has been entrusted to him. In 16:1-13 Jeremiah tells his listeners another personal story that, like the linen loincloth one, has a "message" embedded in it for his people and also for himself.

Again it is God who tells Jeremiah what to do (or not to do): in this case, not to take a wife or have any children in the land of Judah because whole families are about to die from disease, war, and famine. Furthermore, their dead bodies will be "like dung," and will be eaten by birds and wild animals instead of being buried.[4]

Jeremiah's simile is self-explanatory, but he adds to the suspense of the story by next relating what God wants him (not) to do in the face of such tragedy and devastation: he is not to mourn, and those who suffer are not to be offered any comfort or consolation by anyone. God's reason, according to Jeremiah, is simple: God is going to leave the people without any peace at all. Even more devastating is the news Jeremiah receives from God about himself: namely, that he will live to see God take away all joy.

> I am going to banish from this place, in your days and before your eyes,
> the voice of mirth and the voice of gladness, the voice of the bridegroom
> and the voice of the bride. (Jer 16:9)

In the last part of his story Jeremiah repeats to his listeners the "one-way conversation" God had with him, with God hypothetically quoting the Judahites and then telling Jeremiah how he is to respond to the people. Once again it is as if God is letting Jeremiah have some privileged information about the Judahites that he, in turn, now shares with them. And once again the theme of God's and Jeremiah's message to them is the same: they have sinned; they have forsaken God; they are guilty of apostasy—they and their ancestors (and they themselves are even worse than their ancestors). The

---

[4] In the ancient world giving a proper burial was considered to be a righteous act on behalf of someone who had lived a righteous life. To leave someone's dead body out in the fields for the wild animals and birds was a sign that the person was unrighteous and therefore cursed (see Gen 40:19; 1 Sam 17:44-46; cf. Deut 28:26 and elsewhere in Jeremiah: 8:2; 9:22; 14:16; 15:3; 16:3-4; 19:7; 22:18-19, etc.).

reference to the "ancestors" recalls an earlier proclamation of Jeremiah's that pertains to Israel's sinfulness, with Judah implied (see Jer 3:11-25). Key words and repetitive themes emphasize the people's infidelity and the fact that they do not seem to realize that they have broken covenant, as evidenced by the three rhetorical questions in v. 10, which show just how hard-hearted and blind they have become. Jeremiah's last comment foreshadows the loss of land and the exile of those people who survive disease, war, and famine. All of these events did happen historically and were thought to be from the hand of God who, according to Jeremiah, had resolved to show the guilty parties no favor.

The main symbol in this story is Jeremiah in his celibate state. If we view Jeremiah's situation today through the lens of an older understanding of celibacy we can understand how this way of life, commanded by God, leaves Jeremiah spouseless, childless, and "fruitless." Marriage and the ability to procreate and bring forth children were signs of God's blessing and an expression of fertility. Hence, just as Jeremiah will not sow his seed, so God will not sow the land any more. Just as Jeremiah will experience the lack of comfort from a family, so will families lack comfort from Jeremiah and others when they experience the tragedies foreshadowed. There is, however, a positive outcome to Jeremiah's having to embrace a celibate life: he will be spared the suffering of the potential loss of his own family, had he had one, when the great and the small die in the land as God predicts (Jer 16:6). It also leaves him free to be focused solely on his mission.

This story portrays Jeremiah as someone whose life and life choices are being shaped and directed by God. To say that he has no "control" over his life would not be accurate because, after all, he does have the same freedom as his community. He could go his own way, but ultimately he would have no peace (Jer 16:5). God's words to Jeremiah, which apply to his addressees, imply that listening to God and allowing God's ways to become "the way" and the "road less traveled" are the actions that lead to peace. Ultimately that peace will be Jeremiah's gift, but not yet completely, for he has work to do that will cause him grief (see, e.g., Jer 17:14-18; 20:7-18).

The people in the story appear impervious to the great gift Jeremiah is to them. Here he is, telling the people of his day all about what is going to happen to them because of their wicked ways. With this foreknowledge they are afforded an opportunity to make choices that would lead to life and not death (see Deut 30:19-20). Embedded in Jeremiah's foreboding message to his listeners is a vision of hope. Things can be different, if only the people will do the work that needs to be done to retrieve the union with their God they first enjoyed when covenant was young. Preacher of grace, poet of truth, Jeremiah remains faithful to God and to a people who have lost their way.

But the people are so enmeshed in religious infidelity to God that they no longer recognize their transgression. They have lost all perception of themselves, as their own questions show. Thus the story sheds light on both the character Jeremiah and his audience. One can only imagine how infuriated Jeremiah's audience must have been at him and at God when they heard this story, especially because they perceived themselves as innocent (v. 10; cf. Jer 2:35). Then again, they may have been so distanced from themselves they could not even take "to heart" Jeremiah's words.

In this passage the character of God looms large. This God with whom Jeremiah shares an intimate relationship will not tolerate infidelity. The God who speaks to Jeremiah in 16:1-13 is an angry God whose hand will mete out punitive justice. The people will be cursed by God because of their apostasy. God plans to punish them indiscriminately—both the great and the small (v. 6). Here is divine warning of death in the land (v. 4), but also of exile, which at least implies life for some among those living under God's curse:

> Therefore I will hurl you out of this land into a land that neither you nor your ancestors have known, and there you shall serve other gods day and night, for I will show you no favor. (v. 13)

Here is a rhetorical double entendre in "you," alluding to the Babylonian exile of 587 B.C.E. The language shifts from third-person references where death is predicted (vv. 1-7) to second-person pronouns where exile is foreshadowed (v. 13). In the text Jeremiah does not die; he is exiled. One wonders if Jeremiah, separate from and yet part of the community he addresses, sees his own fate foreshadowed in the words he delivers from God.

For audiences today Jeremiah's fidelity to his mission and to his God, with all it costs him, is exemplary. He has not only to proclaim God's word, but also to live it through his own life. Jeremiah's God is portrayed through the lens of the deuteronomistic theology of retribution (see Deuteronomy 28; cf. Deut 30:15-20), and because of this theological construct that influenced the shaping of the prophetic texts, and in particular the book of Jeremiah and Jeremiah the character, the inevitable Babylonian invasion is attributed to God, who neither controls nor dominates the historical scene but instead tries to work with it, as Jeremiah the character exemplifies.

Jeremiah 19:1-15: A Tale about a Broken Earthenware Jug

Similar to the story about the linen loincloth, this one about an earthenware jug that Jeremiah breaks in the presence of some elders of the people and some senior priests also shows Jeremiah's word combined with a symbolic action. Once again Jeremiah tells the people of Judah and Jerusalem about an encounter with God, and again he explains for them not only the content of his experience but also its significance for their fate.

This story, like the others, begins with a typical messenger formula that establishes the credibility of the message and signals to the listeners that they are going to hear something about God. The central symbol this time is an earthenware jug, a familiar object in Jeremiah's day. He buys this jug and holds it before the senior priests and the elders while reciting a series of ominous acts God is going to do, namely: bring judgment on the inhabitants of Judah and Jerusalem, and the city itself in particular, destroying both the inhabitants of Jerusalem and the city itself, like a clay pot that has been smashed, whose pieces are so badly broken that they cannot be glued back together again. The city will be so defiled that it will resemble Topheth, now renamed the Valley of Slaughter (v. 13; cf. v. 6).[5] As Jeremiah tells the story he performs the symbolic action of breaking the pot in front of the people, as God had commanded him to do.

Jeremiah's rhetorical sequence and narrative progression of foreshadowed events add suspense to his story, which climaxes in verse 10 when he breaks the clay pot to get his point across. Jeremiah's reference to the people's dead bodies becoming food for the birds of the air and the wild animals of the earth recalls what he said to them earlier in the story about his celibacy (v. 7; cf. 16:4). His assertion that God accuses the people of apostasy and idolatry is a variation on a now common theme (vv. 4-5; cf. 16:11; Jeremiah 2–4), as is God's threat of punishment, disclosed in Jeremiah's story (cf. also 13:1-11).

Jeremiah's symbols of the clay pot and his symbolic action of smashing it, coupled with a his repetitive statements of divine judgment and his repetition of key phrases and common themes, all point up the baseness of the inhabitants of Jerusalem and Judah and their utter stubbornness (see Jer 5:23; 7:24; 11:8; 16:12; 18:12). Jeremiah's continued use of symbols is a further attempt by Jeremiah and by God to bring the inhabitants of Judah to the realization of their transgressions and so to lay the foundation for their return. But their persistent efforts remain fruitless; there is no indication whatsoever from Jeremiah of the people's change of heart. Furthermore, by symbolically taking some of the elders and senior priests of the community with him when he proclaims his foreboding message, and by singling out the kings of Judah through a vocative (v. 3), Jeremiah indirectly indicts the religious and political leadership of his day for not calling the people back

---

[5] In Jeremiah's time Topheth, in the Valley of Hinnom, was the site of an altar where children were said to have been sacrificed.

to covenant fidelity and Torah. They have become as bad as the inhabitants themselves (vv. 1, 3). Jeremiah's story is a reminder to today's listeners and readers that a prophet is called to be faithful and not successful in carrying out God's vision and mission. Finally, there is no sign or word of hope in this story at all. Even the smashed clay pot, as a symbol, cannot be put back together again. Jeremiah's audience is on a downward course to disaster.

Jeremiah 25:15-31: A Tale about a Cup of Wine

In this next narrative Jeremiah moves his listeners and readers from the local scene to an international one. The main symbol he uses to communicate a picture of the whole world coming apart at the seams is a cup of wine. This cup of wine is a cup of God's wrath. The image is borrowed from stock images in the tradition. What Jeremiah has been foreshadowing and God threatening to do is about to happen: "See, I am beginning to bring disaster on the city that is called by my name. . . . I am summoning a sword against all the inhabitants of the earth, says the LORD of hosts" (v. 29). The details of Jeremiah's story, and all his proclamations, symbols, and symbolic actions, have been leading up to this fateful moment, which begins with a drink from the cup.

The story begins matter-of-factly, like the others. Jeremiah tells his listeners about another encounter he had with God: God offered him a cup, and he took it. Jeremiah then explains how God called this cup "the cup of the wine of wrath," which all nations had to drink: (1) Jerusalem and the towns of Judah, its kings and officials; (2) Pharaoh, king of Egypt, his servants, his officials, and all his people; (3) "all the mixed people"; (4) all the kings of the land of Uz; (5) all the kings of the land of the Philistines—Ashkelon, Gaza, Ekron, and the remnant of Ashdod; (6) Edom; (7) Moab; (8) the Ammonites; (9) all the kings of Tyre; (10) all the kings of Sidon; (11) the kings of the coastlands across the sea; (12) Dedan; (13) Tema; (14) Buz; (15) "all who have shaven temples"; (16) all the kings of Arabia; (17) all the kings of the mixed peoples that live in the desert; (18) all the kings of Zimri; (19) all the kings of Elam; (20) all the kings of Media; (21) all the kings of the north; (22) all the kingdoms of the whole world that are on the face of the earth; and last but not least, after all have drunk, (23) the king of Sheshach, better known as Babylon (vv. 19-26).

By listing one group of people after another Jeremiah verbally dramatizes the extent of the devastation that is now looming on the horizon, which will climax with judgment on Babylon, the greatest of all empires at this time. As three recent commentators observe:

Such a listing moves generally from south to north (the opposite direction of the "foe from the north" oracles). The list also moves from neighboring nations to more distant nations, with Babylon being the climax of the oracle. Thus the list progresses from Egypt on the southwestern border of Judah to Philistia along the southwestern coastal plain, then to the southeastern and eastern border with Edom, Moab, and Ammon. Then the list moves to the northwestern border with Phoenicia and more distant northwestern areas ("the coast across the sea," perhaps Phoenician colonies or Cyprus or the coastal regions of Turkey). Next the list moves again to the eastern regions, this time to those places more distant than Edom, Moab, and Ammon: Arabia and the desert dwellers. Then the list moves to the distant lands beyond the Babylonian homeland: Elam and Media (and presumably the otherwise unknown Zimri). A summary statement follows: all the kings of the north, near and far, and all the kingdoms of the earth drink from the cup. Finally, as the climactic focus of the pericope, the king of Sheshak . . . [Babylon] drinks from the cup.[6]

Furthermore, Jeremiah makes clear to his listeners that this cup of the wine of God's wrath is no ordinary cup of wine that would either bring refreshment or cause drunkenness. It is a wine that will make them rage (v. 16). His allusion to God's sword is metaphorical. The nations are going to go to war against each other, an inevitable evil that is understood as "God's doing" (vv. 16, 27).

Later in his story Jeremiah shifts from referring to God as "the LORD, the God of Israel" to "the LORD of hosts, the God of Israel" (vv. 15, 27). With this descriptive image of God as "the God of hosts" Jeremiah lets his audience know that "warrior God" is behind the foreshadowed destruction; this God's command to the nations is: "Drink, get drunk and vomit, fall and rise no more, because of the sword that I am sending among you" (v. 27). Here Jeremiah has communicated God's intention in graphic and repulsive imagery. Jeremiah next emphasizes that God has given the nations no choice as to whether or not to drink: they must. Finally, Jeremiah quotes God, as he has been doing throughout his story, and reveals to his listeners the plain truth about "the city that is called by [God's] name," a metaphorical reference to Jerusalem:

[6] Peter C. Craigie, Page H. Kelley, and Joel F. Drinkard, Jr., *Jeremiah 1–25*. WBC 26 (Dallas: Word Books, 1991) 371.

> See, I am beginning to bring disaster on the city that is called by my name, and how can you possibly avoid punishment? You shall not go unpunished, for I am summoning a sword against all the inhabitants of the earth, says the LORD of hosts. (Jer 25:29)

The fate of Judah and of the inhabitants of Israel is sealed, confirmed by the rhetorical question.

Then, in the midst of his storytelling, Jeremiah recites a poem in which he reveals to the people that indeed the catastrophic event that is about to occur is all God's doing (vv. 30-31). The battles that will rage and the destruction that will take place are all a sign of God's judgment, initiated with a cup of wine.

In this passage Jeremiah's prose and poetry interface with each other to create one picture: enraged nations soon to be raging against each other, all stirred up by an enraged warrior God who inflamed them with wrath through a drink of wine from a common cup, served to them by God's "servant," Jeremiah. What an incredible picture Jeremiah has sketched out in his story! What a frightening picture of God he has revealed! And yet there is no word from the prophet that hints at his people's attempt at making right their relationship with God, whose rage is now all-encompassing. One can only imagine the pain Jeremiah felt when he did what he did and saw what he saw in this encounter with his God, which was more like a nightmare than a dream. Finally, from a historical perspective Jeremiah's narrative points out that Judah's future is intricately tied to the fate of the other nations and vice versa. What is foretold by Jeremiah did eventually happen, with the southern kingdom destroyed in 587 B.C.E.

Jeremiah 27:1-22: The Sign of the Yoke

> Thus the LORD said to me: "Make yourself a yoke of straps and bars, and put them on your neck." (Jer 27:2)

What a strange command God had given to Jeremiah! Nevertheless, true to his God and to his mission, Jeremiah puts on the yoke without any hesitation, and standing in front of his audience and yoked, he tells them another story about another encounter he had with his God, who revealed to him more news of future impending events. The yoked Jeremiah becomes a symbolic and prophetic sign that coincides with his words, all of it together foreshadowing the Babylonian exile that followed the devastation of Jerusalem and the Southern Kingdom.

As a biblical symbol derived from the agricultural world of ancient times the yoke is an image of subjection, service, and/or bondage associated with both the ox and the donkey, two animals commonly used for labor. Throughout the Bible the yoke was used metaphorically as a sign of political subjection to a foreign ruler (cf. Deut 28:48) or to the nation's own king (1 Kgs 12:4-14). The yoke was also a sign of sin (Lam 1:14) and an indication of a close alliance or union, as when two animals are yoked together.[7] As a central symbol in Jeremiah 27:1-22 the yoke Jeremiah wears functions as a double entendre. It points to the people's further experience of Babylonian captivity as well as their sinfulness, with Jeremiah's focus being on the former.

Jeremiah's account opens with an editorial comment that situates the passage historically (v. 1).[8] Verse 2 begins Jeremiah's report of his divine encounter, related in a prose narrative. Here Jeremiah is seen once again as a great, straightforward storyteller. His story consists of three parts: (1) a divine commissioning that consists of a symbol, a symbolic action, and a message for neighboring kings (vv. 2-11), (2) a message for King Zedekiah of Judah (vv. 12-15), and (3) a message for the priests and all the Judahites (vv. 16-22). Jeremiah's messages to the political and religious leadership of his day are significant. One of the roles of a prophet was to be an advisor to leadership and, when necessary, to call leadership to account with respect to governance; for the Israelite leaders this meant holding them accountable for upholding Torah and covenant throughout the land. Here Jeremiah is seen fulfilling that role as prophet-advisor.

In the first part of his story (vv. 2-11) Jeremiah is commanded to fashion a yoke for himself and to put it on (v. 2). While wearing this yoke (apparently) he is to send a message to neighboring kings via envoys who have come to Jerusalem to King Zedekiah of Judah (v. 3). The message he is to give these envoys is to contain certain information God has dictated (vv. 4-11). In this divine confession God reveals something about God's self and what God intends to do at this stage in the nations' history. Through Jeremiah the neighboring kings meet the God of creation who exercises sovereign power

---

[7] For further study see "Yoke," in Leland Ryken, James C. Wilhoit, and Tremper Longman, III, eds., *Dictionary of Biblical Imagery* (Downers Grove, IL: InterVarsity, 1998) 975.

[8] While the actual dating of this passage cannot be determined definitely, R. E. Clements observes that "the conspiracy to rebel is dated in verse 11 to 'the beginning of the reign of Zedekiah'. . . . The meeting, however, must have taken place a little later than this and so must probably be dated to the years 594–593 B.C. when Nebuchadnezzar led a military campaign into Syria. . . . We must conclude that chapter 27 represents a narrative compilation written down at some distance in time after the events it recounts had transpired." (See his *Jeremiah*. Interpretation [Atlanta: John Knox, 1988] 160.)

and will do whatever is the divine pleasure (v. 5). They also learn of their fate and that of their respective kingdoms: namely, that Israel's God of creation and LORD of history will deliver these neighboring nations into the hands of Nebuchadnezzar, king of Babylon, thus making Babylon the most powerful of all empires (vv. 6-10). Babylon's greatness, however, is not to be forever. Jeremiah also gives the kings a word of hope. Eventually the tables will be turned and Babylon will become the slave of many nations and kings (v. 7b). God, depicted as the all-powerful deity, intends to bring the most powerful empire to its knees and, in so doing, to liberate the other nations from its ravenous hold.

In verses 8-11 Jeremiah focuses his listeners' attention on the yoke around his neck by announcing that God has also said that anyone who goes against the divine plan to have the nations submit to the Babylonians will be punished by God, and that the people are not to listen to any prophet or sage who gives advice contrary to what God has spoken. At this point submission by the nations will mean life for them and not death. Arrogant Babylon with its insatiable appetite for more land, more peoples, more power, and more control will be dealt with once and for all by God, whose power is stronger than any power on earth (cf. Jer 50–51).

The second part of Jeremiah's story is directed toward King Zedekiah of Judah (vv. 12-15). Here Jeremiah indicates that it has been revealed to him that God has already spoken to Zedekiah.[9] For those listening to Jeremiah, and for Jeremiah as well, it has become clear that God has had a direct and active role in the reign of one of Judah's kings. Thus the gift of prophecy continues to be associated with the monarchy as it was in the days of David (see, e.g., 1 Sam 16:12-13). Included in Jeremiah's message to Zedekiah is an instruction concerning false prophets. Here, as in verses 9-10, Jeremiah is indirectly elucidating a problem that exists in his time—false prophecy (see Jer 28)—and he depicts God as aware of the situation while trying to get a handle on the problem by steering the people away from listening to such prophets. Simultaneously God is shown trying to bring Judah into line with what the other nations are to do in the face of the Babylonians. The rhetorical question in verse 13 makes this clear and gives Zedekiah no choice but to lead the people in the way of God's plan. What is significant here is that God speaks directly to Zedekiah and tells him what he must do. Many of the Judahites have not listened to the prophet thus far, so now perhaps the king will be able to get them to respond for the sake of their lives. This

---

[9] The main speaker in verse 12 of Jeremiah's narrative is not Jeremiah; it is God. This section of the story is a continuation of God's speech begun in verse 2 (cf. v. 4).

part of the narrative confirms the prophet's experience, namely, that the prophet is called to be faithful and not successful.

The last part of Jeremiah's story (vv. 16-22) shifts speaker and addressees. Here Jeremiah relates how he went and spoke God's word to the priests and to all the people.[10] This shift in speaker is signaled by the temporal time marker, "then," followed by the messenger formula, both of which are absent in verse 12, where God addresses the king.

Jeremiah tells the priests and people that, like Zedekiah and the kings of the neighboring nations, they are not to listen to any of their own prophets, because these prophets will be prophesying falsely. How ironic! Here is Jeremiah, saying to the priests and the peoples, "Thus says the LORD," asking them to pay attention to him and his message, while at the same time he is telling them not to listen to their prophets who will be telling them something contrary to what he himself is proclaiming, both to them and to the kings of the other nations. The priests and all the people would, perhaps, experience Zedekiah their king ignoring the prophets in order to bring his people into submission to the Babylonians. This movement would be in concert with Jeremiah's message from God to them: ". . . serve the king of Babylon and live" (v. 17), and would confirm Jeremiah as a true prophet. Unfortunately, this does not happen, as history will reveal, and Jeremiah's further predictions to Zedekiah about himself and Jerusalem are fulfilled instead. As in verses 12-15, this section turns on Jeremiah's rhetorical question in verse 17. The city will in fact become a desolation. A final sentence predicts the restoration of the vessels to Jerusalem at the time of the city's restoration.

Jeremiah, faithful to God and his vocation, is a foil for the people and their infidelity. Jeremiah is also God's message dramatized. But because the people have forsaken their God and given their hearts to other gods they will not be able to take Jeremiah's message to heart, nor will they be able to understand his symbolic action. In their wayward state what seems true to them is really false, and what seems false is really true. They have also been influenced by the Zion tradition. Jerusalem is God's holy city and they are God's holy people. Surely nothing will happen to their city or to them. History proves otherwise (see Jer 39:1-10). The passage also sheds light on God, whose image reflects the influence of a royal theology that flows from the monarchal tradition. God, as King of kings, is seen here trying to get a handle on the world scene. At stake is God's sovereign power over all the earth, and thus God makes tactful plans toward leveling the greatest threat

[10] Zedekiah does not listen to Jeremiah's word and receives the reward Jeremiah predicted for him and Jerusalem: he does not escape from the Babylonians' hand, he is abused physically, and Jerusalem is burned (see Jer 38:1–39:10).

of all, the Babylonians. When they are defeated, all will know Israel's God to be "LORD of all." Unfortunately, there is much violence embedded in the message of this text. Such violence reflects the beliefs and culture of an ancient world.

Jeremiah 32:1-15: The Purchase of a Field

This narrative is the last in a series that has featured Jeremiah either as a symbol or performing a symbolic deed. In this passage he buys a field, which foreshadows the resettlement of the Israelites in the land. For a people facing total devastation and the loss of their land, Judah and God's holy city Jerusalem, this message and the deed accompanying it would have been a source of great strength and hope in the midst of their pain if only they had eyes to see, ears to hear, and hearts to remember.

This narrative consists of three smaller units: setting and background (vv. 2-5); divine proclamation and its fulfillment (vv. 6-8); description of Jeremiah's land purchase and symbolic gesture explained (vv. 9-15); and a superscription (v. 1) that is linked to the first unit. This purchasing of land has deep ramifications for the Israelite people, the extent of which will come clear in light of the discussion of verse 15.

The opening verse of the first unit—the superscription—provides a historical framework for the narrative. The references to King Zedekiah and Nebuchadnezzar signal that the end of the Southern Kingdom is near and the Babylonian invasion is close at hand. Zedekiah was the last of Israel's kings to rule in Judah. These two references also hark back to the story of Jeremiah and the yoke (see Jer 27:1, 6, 12), which helps to create narrative unity between the stories and a sense of narrative progression among these "sign" stories as a whole.

The backdrop for this narrative is Jeremiah's encounter with Zedekiah, which the text narrates in past and past present tense. Verses 2-5 provide a glimpse into the kind of relationship Jeremiah had with Zedekiah. Confined in Zedekiah's court of the guard, which was in the king's palace, Jeremiah exchanges words with the king. Zedekiah's pointed questions and comments to Jeremiah indicate the king's discomfort with Jeremiah's prophecy. The fact that Zedekiah asks Jeremiah "Why do you prophesy?" is also a clear indication that Jeremiah was seen as a prophet in his day.

Jeremiah responds as if he had not heard the question. Instead of answering directly, he launches into a story about how he had come to buy property. In this story within a story God tells Jeremiah that his cousin is going to come to him to ask that Jeremiah buy his field (v. 7). What God had said comes to pass, and Jeremiah comments: "Then I knew that this was the word of the LORD" (v. 8). Jeremiah is revealed here as an astute person who, in the midst of false prophets, listens to and discerns the spirit of God who has predicted an event to him. Jeremiah has now gained more knowledge about his God and about himself as well. God's word is truthful and will be fulfilled.

Having discerned the spirit behind God's word, Jeremiah then goes and buys the field. In verses 9-14 he carefully lays out the steps he took to secure and safeguard the purchase of the land. Significantly, in the presence of the Judeans Jeremiah hands over the deeds, telling Baruch to put them in an earthenware jug. Here Jeremiah has given the people of Judah symbol after symbol. First, the purchase of the field indicates that their land, soon to be captured and ravished, will be restored to them. Second, the signing of the deeds in their presence indicates that they will be given the rights to the land once again. Third, the command to Baruch to put the deeds in an earthenware jug "in order that they may last for a long time" reverses the imagery of Jeremiah 19:1-15 where an earthenware jar, symbolizing the people of Judah, is smashed beyond repair. His final word, cast as a proclamation that follows a messenger formula, explains clearly the meaning behind his symbolic action of land purchase:

> For thus says the LORD of hosts, the God of Israel: Houses and fields
> and vineyards shall again be bought in this land. (v. 15)

Jeremiah knows God's word is true and will come to pass. Thus he gives a vision of hope to those listening to him. But if they do not hear or believe in his proclamations of disaster, how will they ever hear him now? Estranged from their God, they are also estranged from perceiving the subtle events that are happening around them that, for them, will come as a surprise, especially when they lose all, but not so for Jeremiah who has the double vision of the prophet—to see the horror and the beauty at the heart of transformation. What must be remembered, however, is that the way this transformation happens is reflective of a culture and a theology colored by the culture and, in some ways, wedded to that culture. From a present-day theological perspective a change of heart and the ongoing change of life on the planet may have violence as a means to an end, but this violence must be held up for ongoing critical theological reflection.

This narrative in its entirety makes clear that

> . . . while this is a carefully performed, economic, legal act, it is not an
> economic or legal transaction. It is a land deal freighted with enormous

theological significance. . . . The entire process of vv. 6-15 holds together the theological reality of God's promise and the restoration of
an economic infrastructure.[11]

For the people of Israel the future is bright, but not until they have the
devastating yet purifying experience of losing all fruit.

In Retrospect . . .

Beginning with the narrative of the linen loincloth and concluding with
the one about the purchase of a field, Jeremiah's stories have provided snap-
shots of events that loom on the horizon of his world. Collectively Jeremiah
13:1-11; 16:1-13; 19:1-15 build up to the climactic story in 25:15-31, with
27:1-22 and 32:1-15 foreshadowing events that will take place after the fall
of Jerusalem and the collapse of Judah. Each of these narratives contains either
a major symbol, a symbolic action performed by Jeremiah, or both, crucial
elements of drama as God and Jeremiah try time and again to capture their
audience's attention audio-visually. These narratives are a testament to the
creative genius of Jeremiah who, inspired by God, combines symbolic gestures
with rhetorical artistry that can be poetic, prosaic, or both. What Jeremiah
has done in these narratives is to take common, ordinary elements from a
community's daily life experience, connect these elements to the signs of
the times, and, with a theological lens, reinterpret the ordinary elements in
light of the life of a community and its historical times. Jeremiah has created
symbols, and the creative genius of God has made Jeremiah into a living
symbol through whom the word of God comes alive and shines transparently.
Jeremiah's life incarnates God's word, and in the process Jeremiah becomes
not only a prophet to the people but also a prophet of God.

---

[11] Walter Brueggemann, *A Commentary on Jeremiah: Exile and Homecoming* (Grand
Rapids: Eerdmans, 1998) 301.

CHAPTER FOUR

In Conversation with God

Introduction

Characters in a book become known to their readers not only by what they say but also by how they relate to and interact with other characters. The two main characters in the book of Jeremiah, as has been seen thus far, are Jeremiah and God. God, who knew Jeremiah before he was formed in the womb, and who consecrated him before he was born, has a wonderful and intimate relationship with the prophet. Jeremiah, called and commissioned by God, is shown to be faithful to God and to his mission as a prophet. What is interesting to observe is how these two characters "interface" with each other. Each candidly challenges the other. Between God and Jeremiah exists a deep level of trust and a great love for God's people. This trust and love moves Jeremiah to proclaim God's word to a variety of people in his community, most of whom reject both the word and Jeremiah. Through Jeremiah's experiences with his God and with the people of his community we see how the prophet develops in stamina and grows in wisdom.

Jeremiah 4:9-10: Deceived by God?

Who would ever think of indicting God? Who would ever suggest that God is a liar? And who would ever dare to confront God about certain ways that suggest God is deceptive? Jeremiah, bold, courageous, and assertive, has a rather curt conversation with God. Cast in prose, the conversation between God and Jeremiah opens with God making a statement about what is to occur in the future:

> On that day, says the LORD, courage shall fail the king and the officials;
> the priests shall be appalled and the prophets astounded. (4:9)

Jeremiah responds:

> "Ah, Lord GOD, how utterly you have deceived this people and Jeru-
> salem, saying, 'It shall be well with you,' even while the sword is at
> the throat!" (4:10)

God has declared to Jeremiah that the political and religious leadership
of his day—the king, the officials, the priests, and the prophets—will soon
be rendered ineffective. The phrase "on that day" refers to the Day of the
LORD, which will be a day of judgment, unlike the times of the Exodus when
it was a day of deliverance and salvation. The implied reference here is to
the military invasion by the Babylonians that will soon take place.

Jeremiah's response to God is direct and honest. First, he accuses God
of being deceptive, and second, he quotes God to point out the inconsistency
of God's words. A people once told by God that all shall be well are now
hearing that their leadership will fail them. The irony, as Jeremiah points
out, is that God makes this statement in the face of looming military invasion. Although Jeremiah is quite disappointed with God for having seemingly
deceived the people, God's opening phrase, "On that day" does point to the
grim days ahead and, although there will be much bloodshed, ironically in
the end "all shall be well" despite the sword at the throat, because some
people's lives will be spared; the nation will survive.

The fact that Jeremiah is reporting this conversation to the people of
his day, and speaking as if God is speaking through him, provides one with
an insight into how the prophet viewed the leadership of his time: unable to
anticipate the looming crisis. Indirectly he blames God for this situation,
since God is the one who is supposed to be working with and through leadership by way of divine election and divine inspiration. Thus Jeremiah makes
a strong indictment against the royal theology of his day.

Jeremiah 5:1-19: O LORD, Do Your Eyes Not Look for Truth?

In this graphic conversation between God and Jeremiah, God speaks
candidly to Jeremiah and vice versa. Neither character minces any words, and
Jeremiah makes a few rather disconcerting with regard to people's economic
class. Again God bluntly lays out the people's faults, and Jeremiah, delivering
the entire message to his audience, paints for them a vivid picture of why
God is so adamant against them. If only they had ears to hear!

The passage can be divided into four subunits: God's statement to
Jeremiah (vv. 1-2), Jeremiah's response to God (v. 3), Jeremiah's personal

reflection (vv. 4-6), and God's further statement to Jeremiah (vv. 7-19). In the first subunit God challenges Jeremiah to find someone in the community who is just and truthful so that the community, through that person, could receive pardon:

> Run to and fro through the streets
> > of Jerusalem,
> look around and take note!
> Search its squares and see
> > if you can find one person
> who acts justly
> > and seeks truth—
> so that I may pardon Jerusalem. (v. 1)

God is also quick to point out to Jeremiah the people's hypocrisy:

> Although they say, "As the LORD lives,"
> > yet they swear falsely. (v. 2)

This technique of quoting the community sheds light on God as one who "knows," and in this case knows the people's duplicity. The irony in God's statement to Jeremiah is that Jeremiah is one person who acts justly and seeks truth, and yet it is as if God is blind to him. The double irony is the fact that Jeremiah is standing before his community, proclaiming these words, and his community does not realize his just and truthful presence among them, through which they could return to God and be saved. They are blind, as God seems to be, to Jeremiah's righteous life.

Jeremiah's response to God is just as ironic:

> O LORD, do your eyes not look for truth?
> You have struck them,
> > but they felt no anguish;
> you have consumed them,
> > but they refused to take correction.
> They have made their faces harder than rock;
> > they have refused to turn back. (v. 3)

It almost seems as though Jeremiah is not picking up on God's candor. God has challenged Jeremiah to try to find one decent living and faithful person in the community; Jeremiah retorts with a rhetorical question that is itself ironic (v. 3a), and then blurts out to God what God has done to the people and how they have been unresponsive to God's action. The poet's use of antithesis points up not only the harshness of God's chastisement but also the hardness of the people, who refuse to return to God. But having been dealt a blow by God and having been consumed as well, who would turn back to this God? Jeremiah's response confirms how deserving of divine judgment the community is. In all this it is important to keep in mind the cultural and theological perspective that shaped the poet's, people's, and later editor's understanding of historical events.

Nudged by God's challenge, Jeremiah begins his search in the squares to see if he can find one upright person:

> Then I said, "These are only the poor,
>   they have no sense;
> for they do not know the way of the LORD,
>   the law of their God.
> Let me go to the rich
>   and speak to them;
> surely they know the way of the LORD,
>   the law of their God."
> But they all alike had broken the yoke,
>   they had burst the bonds. (vv. 4-5)

Here the poet shares his inner thoughts with his audience. He has searched among the poor and the rich only to discover the infidelity of both, which he expresses in metaphorical language. The yoke to which he refers has a different nuance than the one he wore around his neck to symbolize the foreshadowing of the people's captivity (Jer 27:8).[1] This yoke in 5:5 is associated with service to God (Jer 2:20). Metaphorically, however, both nuances of "yoke" communicate a similar idea: the people are subservient, whether to a foreign king or to God. Furthermore, from a hermeneutical perspective Jeremiah's economic class distinction in relation to knowledge is derogatory and brings to light the general unjust attitude toward the poor in his day.

Having found no righteous person, Jeremiah describes metaphorically what the people's fate will be. His use of animal imagery indicates the savageness of an invading enemy who will prey on the community and its structures until there is nothing left of either.

---

[1] See also the references to "yoke" in relation to Egyptian oppression (Lev 26:13).

> Therefore a lion from the forest shall kill them,
>> a wolf from the desert shall destroy them.
> A leopard is watching against their cities;
>> everyone who goes out of them shall be torn in pieces—
> because their transgressions are many,
>> their apostasies are great. (v. 6)

For ancient people the lion was the fiercest of all animals, ruthless, lying in ambush—ready to strike with boldness and ferocity. People in the ancient world thought that God sometimes used lions as agents of divine chastisement (see, e.g., 1 Kgs 13:26; 20:36; 2 Kgs 17:25). Those thought to be "wicked" were known as "lions" (see, e.g., Pss 7:2; 10:9; 17:12: 22:13, 21; 35:17; 57:4; 58:6; Isa 5:29; Jer 4:7; 50:17). Wolves were also considered ravenous predators that would tear at and devour their prey (see, e.g., Gen 49:27; Ezek 22:27). The leopard was another rapacious beast that lurked, waiting to spring (Dan 7:6). These three animals symbolize judgment, an act signaled by the conjunction "therefore." Walter Brueggemann writes that the metaphors may point to the devastation of an invading army, or perhaps the images refer directly to the coming of YHWH. Either way, juridical language has been transposed into the law of the jungle. Disobedient Jerusalem is at the mercy of vicious beasts (cf. Lev 26:22).[2]

Finally, the poet's use of synonymous parallelism draws attention to the people's waywardness as the reason for the foreboding judgment: "because their transgressions are many, their apostasies are great" (v. 6c).

The last unit of the passage consists of four proclamations: verses 7-9, 10-11, 12-17, and 18-19. Each proclamation adds indictment to indictment against the people and includes a metaphorical description of Babylon (vv. 15b-17), but true to prophetic theology, it contains a message of hope (vv. 18-19). The role of speaker shifts from Jeremiah to God.

Having heard Jeremiah's personal reflections, along with his earlier question, God now responds to Jeremiah with two rhetorical questions, the reverse of the one posed at the beginning of the unit: "How can I pardon you? (v. 7) and "Shall I not punish them for these things? (v. 9). "You" applies not only to Jeremiah as the addressee but also, and more explicitly, to Jeremiah's community, with which he is in solidarity. Once again the crime they have committed is apostasy, described metaphorically as adultery. This adulterous state becomes even more vivid through the use of animal imagery directed at the men of the community:

---

[2] Walter Brueggemann, *A Commentary on Jeremiah: Exile & Homecoming* (Grand Rapids: Eerdmans, 1998) 63.

They were well-fed lusty stallions, each neighing for his neighbor's
wife. (v. 8)

Here again Brueggemann offers a comment on the images found in this
verse:

> The image of "lusty stallions" severely alludes to sexual infidelity and
> perversion, but it is also a metaphor for shameless self-assertion. Judah
> is too full of self. "Horses" in the OT are regularly found only among
> those who, like kings, assert their own power and seize initiative for
> their own lives. This same fullness of self-sufficiency, which leads to
> moral disorientation, also leads to religious self-destruction through
> the mocking of God (Jer 5:12-13).[3]

In verses 10-11 God gives Jeremiah a command:

> Go up through her vine-rows and destroy,
>   but do not make a full end;
> strip away her branches,
>   for they are not the LORD's.
> For the house of Israel and the house of Judah
>   have been utterly faithless to me,
>   says the LORD.

Again Jeremiah is commanded to perform a symbolic action meant to
indict Israel and Judah visually while offering the people a glimmer of hope:
"but do not make a full end" (v. 10a). Jeremiah's incomplete destruction of
the vineyard foreshadows what God intends to do: "But even in those days,
says the LORD, I will not make a full end of you" (v. 18). Surviving will be
the faithful remnant of which Jeremiah is a part. In delivering this divine
proclamation, Jeremiah is really announcing his own fate. He will be spared
just as he spares some of the vineyard.

Verses 12-17 report the people's self-indictment:

> They have spoken falsely of the LORD,
>   and have said, "He will do nothing.
> No evil will come upon us,
>   and we shall not see sword or famine." (v. 12)

---

[3] Ibid. 64.

The inherent irony is obvious: they *will* see the sword and famine. "They" refers not only to the people but also to their prophets (those who oppose and denounce Jeremiah).

> The prophets are nothing but wind,
> for the word is not in them.
> Thus it shall be done to them! (v. 13)

"Therefore," opening verse 14, signals judgment (cf. v. 6), and the use of contrast sets Jeremiah apart from the rest of the prophets who have compromised their prophetic office:

> Because they have spoken this word,
> I am now making my words in your mouth a fire,
> and this people wood, and the fire shall devour them.
> I am going to bring upon you
> a nation from far away,
> O house of Israel,
> says the LORD.

The central image in verses 13-14 is the "word." The prophets' false "word" leads God to make the divine word like fire in Jeremiah's mouth. The word the prophet will speak will be confrontation and exposing of the people's waywardness. Thus Jeremiah contrasts with the prophets of his day, and his word will be the complete opposite of what people want to hear, for it will be a word of judgment. This word of judgment speaks of a nation far away that God will bring upon the house of Israel for its destruction. Here the house of Israel includes both Israel and Judah.

In verses 15b-17 the nation alluded to in v. 15a now becomes the focal point of the unit, as evidenced by the triple use of the keyword "nation" (v. 15 [4x]). It is without doubt that the enduring, ancient nation is Babylon. The metaphorical description of the foreign nation's quiver in verse 16 accents its strength. Verse 17 uses the imagery of "eating up," which harks back to verse 6, where the lion, wolf, and leopard are first introduced. The Babylonians—the lion, wolf, and leopard—are about to ravage the people and their land. The repetitive use of the third-person future tense, "they shall," adds an emphatic ring to God's message as proclaimed by Jeremiah. Although the impending military invasion will cause much pain and damage, not all will be lost. The final two verses of God's response to Jeremiah offer both the prophet and the people a ray of hope:

But even in those days, says the LORD, I will not make a full end of you. And when your people say, "Why has the LORD our God done all these things to us?" you shall say to them, "As you have forsaken me and served foreign gods in your land, so you shall serve strangers in a land that is not yours." (vv. 18-19)

God's final word is hopeful. Destruction will not be complete. Judah's fate is exile, not extinction.

In Retrospect . . .

The conversation between God and Jeremiah as reported by Jeremiah is one that reveals to past and present audiences a picture of Israel's God as a God of punitive tit-for-tat justice who remains angry at the people for their infidelity. This God is intuitive, knowing the people's thoughts and later quoting them. This God is very powerful and imaginative, one who has set Jeremiah up as a prophet to the prophets and the people of his day. Jeremiah has a strong sense of self in the face of this God, and does not hesitate to raise questions as he ponders the situation of Israel and Judah that leads him to conclude that God's judgment is justified. Finally, Jeremiah is the one under God's command and charged by God to preach both an alarming message and a message of hope. God's final word and the prophet's are one and the same: there will be a deliverance from the hand of the enemy; there will be an exile, but not annihilation. The imagery used reflects the people's agrarian culture, and the picture of God is, once again, conditioned by the history, culture, and theology of the day.

CHAPTER FIVE

*Persistence and Courage
in the Face of Opposition and Threat*

Introduction

Besides his frequent interfacing with God, Jeremiah also interacts with a variety of people in his community, many of them in positions of leadership. Whether prophesying in the Temple, confronting the false prophet Hananiah, or enduring imprisonment and being thrown into a cistern, Jeremiah stands tall and remains in conversation with his God and with those most opposed to him. This chapter portrays Jeremiah "interfacing" with a wide number of personalities, all of whom shed further light on the prophet. Their words and deeds also reveal something about themselves as the vocation, mission, and character of Jeremiah continue to unfold.

Jeremiah 20:1-6: "Terror-all-around"

Jeremiah, God's fortified city, iron pillar, and bronze wall (1:18) was no stranger to physical violence incurred because of his work as a prophet. The story of Jeremiah's encounter with Pashhur is one of the first instances in which Jeremiah interfaces with a religious leader opposed to his work as a prophet. Pashhur, a priest and son of Immer, a chief officer in the house of the Lord, heard Jeremiah's prophecy against Jerusalem, its towns, and all the inhabitants (v. 1). Jeremiah's proclamation causes Pashhur to act negatively toward Jeremiah: he strikes him and puts him in stocks (v. 2). Pashhur's behavior reflects the culture of his day as well as Jewish law. Louis Stulman points out that

> as chief officer in charge of policing the temple for troublemakers and madmen (see also 29:26), Pashhur, in all likelihood, acts only in

accordance with the Deuteronomic law when he beats and imprisons Jeremiah. Deuteronomy 25:2-3 orders flogging for the party at fault in litigation disputes, and there are considerable grounds for reading the altercation as a legal dispute. In his role as temple overseer responsible for maintaining order, the priest is to thwart any attempt to violate existing systems of control. His intense opposition to Jeremiah, although misguided and injudicious, makes sense, for Jeremiah dares to speak against the state's treasured ideologies and institutions.[1]

Jeremiah offers no reaction, response, or act of retaliation to Pashhur's direct attack on him.

The subsequent sequence of events unfolds gradually in the narrative. The temporal reference "the next day" (v. 3), which introduces the next part of the narrative, indicates that Jeremiah spent the whole night in stocks. Pashhur releases Jeremiah after his overnight ordeal, but the violence done to him does not stop him from performing the duties of his task as prophet: he prophesies against Pashhur (vv. 3-6). Pashhur does not respond; Jeremiah, as prophet, has had the last word.

Jeremiah 21:1-10: Thus You Shall Say to Zedekiah

One of Jeremiah's tasks as a prophet was to give advice to the ruling line of his day, and the kings, for their part, often sought out the prophets to learn about the intentions of the gods. In this narrative King Zedekiah sends Pashhur son of Malchiah and the priest Zephaniah son of Maaseiah to Jeremiah. Zedekiah is aware that King Nebuchadnezzar of Babylon is making war against Judah, and Zedekiah desires a word from God concerning the situation. Zedekiah, tempted by Egypt, is hoping that God will act on his and his people's behalf (vv. 1-2).

The narrative provides no further details except to relate what Jeremiah says to Pashhur and Zephaniah by way of a "message" to King Zedekiah. God's "word" to the king and the people is not altogether positive. Warfare and devastation are imminent, but if the Judeans leave Jerusalem and surrender to the Babylonians, the Judeans' lives will be spared (vv. 3-10). Jeremiah's word from God to Zedekiah and the people is far from what the king would have hoped for, but Jeremiah does not try to find favor with the king. Instead, he remains true to himself and true to his God, and he places

---

[1] Louis Stulman, *Jeremiah.* Abingdon Old Testament Commentaries (Nashville: Abingdon, 2005) 195.

Pashhur and Zephaniah in a difficult position: they must deliver a woeful message to their king, and a message containing a choice to their people.

On a literary level this narrative serves as a "hinge that holds together rhetorical sections denouncing priest, prophet, shepherd (king), and sage, namely, major shareholders in the old world order (18:18–20:18 and 21:11–23:40)."[2] Historically and theologically, Jeremiah's message makes clear that the Davidic monarchy is on the brink of disaster and possible extinction, especially since Zedekiah, who is about to receive a grave message from God, is the last king of the Davidic line. The horrible death of Zedekiah at the hands of his enemies will not, however, be the end of the Davidic monarchy (52:10-11). Zedekiah's death will signify the end of an old world order and the emergence of a new one as God had promised and as Jeremiah had announced earlier (23:5-8).

Jeremiah 26:1-24: Stand in the Court of the Lord's House

This wonder-filled prose narrative is the story of Jeremiah's experience in the court of the Temple, where he delivered God's word only to meet with stiff resistance from religious and political leaders as well as the people of Judah, who first call for his life and then later change their minds. A tale within a tale reveals a not-so-positive experience for another prophet, Uriah, who, like Jeremiah, proclaims a foreboding word to the people and their leaders. Not so lucky as Jeremiah, Uriah is forced to flee for his life.

This narrative about Jeremiah's Temple prophecies can be subdivided into six units: (1) God's instructions to Jeremiah and Jeremiah's Temple speech (vv. 1-6), (2) the response of Judah's religious leadership (vv. 7-9), (3) the political leadership's response to the events thus far (vv. 10-15), (4) the collaborative decision of the people and their leaders (vv. 16-19), (5) a story about the prophet Uriah (vv. 20-23), and (6) an editorial comment (v. 24).

The story about Jeremiah's experience in the court of the Temple opens with a historical reference to the beginning of the reign of King Jehoiakim, son of Josiah of Judah (v. 1). Jehoiakim became king in 609 B.C.E. In verses 2-6 Jeremiah reports what God has told him to do. He is to: (1) stand in the court of the Lord's house, (2) speak to the people of all the cities of Judah who came to worship in the Temple, and (3) speak all God's words, not holding back one. The three imperatives "stand," "speak," (twice), and "do not hold back" create a sense of urgency and definitiveness. Jeremiah must do what God asks him to do. Ultimately God holds out hope that the people

---

[2] Ibid. 205.

will listen to Jeremiah, turn from their wicked ways, and so enable God to change God's mind about bringing disaster on the people (v. 3). Jeremiah next reports on what God told him to say to the people. The message is ominous. If the people will not respond to the prophet and amend their ways, the Temple will be made "like Shiloh" and the city of Jerusalem a "curse" (v. 6). "Like Shiloh" sends a strong message to Jeremiah's listeners. J. A. Thompson notes:

> The particular judgment intended for the temple was not to make it like the ancient sanctuary at Shiloh (1 Sam 1–4). Shiloh was evidently destroyed about 1050 B.C. by the Philistine incursion into the land referred to in 1 Sam 4. There is archeological evidence to support this (cf. Ps 78:60, 61). Shiloh may have been rebuilt later but was again destroyed. It was in ruins in Jeremiah's day and constituted a vivid picture of the destruction that was intended for Jerusalem and the temple.[3]

The next part of the narrative describes the religious leaders' appalled response to Jeremiah's proclamation. Their own indictment of him—"You shall die!"—followed by their accusatory question in which they quote his words are indications of their outright hostility. Additionally, that the Temple become like Shiloh was unthinkable. This was God's Temple in God's holy city. The Zion Tradition informed them that both Temple and city were under God's protection. The irony here is that neither the priests nor the other prophets are able to perceive the truth in Jeremiah's words that sheds light on their wayward state. They too have sunk into the complacency of believing in old traditions without realizing that God's foremost concern is not a building or a city, but a relationship rooted in fidelity.

Following Jeremiah's proclamation, and after the negative response of priests, prophets, and people, the next group introduced into the story includes Judah's officials—the political leaders who give a hearing to the priests and prophets who beg to pass sentence on Jeremiah (vv. 10-11).

With many assembled around him, calling for his death, Jeremiah finally speaks on his own behalf. He acknowledges that God has sent him to prophesy against the Temple, city, and people, and then proceeds to tell the people to amend their ways so that divine salvation may be theirs. In verse 14 he shifts his audience's attention to himself through the use of a *casus pendens,* "as for me." He does not resist these people asking for his life, but he makes it clear to them that he is innocent. In his address to Judah's leaders and people one hears Jeremiah's assertiveness and strong sense of self.

---

[3] J. A. Thompson, *The Book of Jeremiah* (Grand Rapids: Eerdmans, 1980) 525.

Such self-possessed comments generate a further response from leadership, now including the elders of the people. These elders, having a sense of history and an understanding of the prophetic tradition (they quote from the prophet Micah), redirect the thinking of the other leaders and the people, with the result that Jeremiah's life is spared. These elders thus represent Israel's "wisdom" tradition.

Verses 20-23 are a digression from the flow of the main story and reveal Jeremiah's good fortune. Uriah the prophet, even though he spoke the same words as Jeremiah, is put to death, but Jeremiah survives:

> But the hand of Ahikam son of Shaphan was with Jeremiah so that he
> was not given over into the hands of the people to be put to death.
> (v. 24)

The divine promise made to Jeremiah at the time of his call and commission—"I am with you, says the LORD, to deliver you" (Jer 1:19)—remains constant. Perhaps Jeremiah was able to stand up to his adversaries because he knew and remembered God's promise. But the people, despite Jeremiah's proclamations to them, remain impervious to his words; they fail to realize that the prophetic words of Micah quoted by the elders will come to pass in Judah. Within the community there is no knowledge and no wisdom. They have gone far from God, the source of all knowledge and wisdom, and even Jeremiah cannot bring them to their senses and a change of heart. Thus the elders' reading of the situation, past and present, is inaccurate. God has not changed God's mind; the destruction is just slow in coming as God holds out chance after chance to a people who will, in fact, bring disaster upon themselves.

This brief narrative about Jeremiah's experience in the court of the Temple has given later readers and hearers of this text an insight into the community of Judah and has shed light on how dysfunctional leadership can become when it is no longer attuned to the source of all power, wisdom, understanding, and knowledge. Finally, it offers the reminder that not all prophets are as fortunate as Jeremiah. Some do suffer and die at the hands of oppressive leaders, a reality that calls for the waters of justice to rain down.

Jeremiah 28:1-17: Listen, Hananiah, The LORD Has Not Sent You

Jeremiah 28:1-17 is a fast-paced narrative featuring a lively exchange between Jeremiah and another prophet, Hananiah, whom Jeremiah discredits. Following the editorial comments that provide a setting for the narrative, and Hananiah's first proclamation (vv. 1-4), the give and take between Jeremiah and Hananiah takes place in four stages (vv. 5-9, 10-11, 12-14, 15-16). A final editorial remark draws the narrative to a close (v. 17).

Hananiah's opening prophecy, which he delivers in the Temple in the presence of the priests and all the people, sets the stage for Jeremiah's robust response. Hananiah begins his prophecy with the typical messenger formula, "thus says the LORD of hosts, the God of Israel" (v. 2) and then proceeds to outline God's plan. Hananiah announces that God: (1) has broken the yoke of the king of Babylon (v. 2); (2) will bring back all the vessels of the LORD's house that were taken to Babylon (v. 3); (3) will bring back to Jerusalem all the exiles who went from Judah to Babylon (v. 4); and (4) will break the yoke of the king of Babylon (v. 4). The first time the breaking of the yoke is mentioned, it is announced in the past tense as if it has already happened. This rhetorical device is known as the prophetic perfect or the tense of vision. Hananiah's prophecy is a direct challenge to one of Jeremiah's earlier prophecies (see Jer 27:16-22). It is optimistic and upbeat, and it puts a positive tone on the ominous invasion by the Babylonians. His message conflicts with that of Jeremiah, whose central theme is doom. Jeremiah offers Hananiah a candid but ironic response:

> Amen! May the LORD do so; may the LORD fulfill the words that you have prophesied, and bring back to this place from Babylon the vessels of the house of the LORD, and all the exiles. (v. 6)

"But . . ."—Jeremiah continues by adjuring Hananiah to listen to the word he is about to speak. He first recalls the words of former prophets who prophesied war, famine, and pestilence against countries and kingdoms. Then he indirectly indicts Hananiah with an invective comment that begins with a *casus pendens:*

> As for the prophet who prophesies peace, when the word of that prophet comes true, then it will be known that the LORD has truly sent the prophet. (v. 9)

Jeremiah has put Hananiah on notice. Hananiah, however, is not going to let Jeremiah have the last word if he can help it. The narrator now portrays Hananiah performing a symbolic action: he breaks the yoke from Jeremiah's neck and then proceeds to offer another proclamation that explains the symbolism of what he has just done:

> "Thus says the LORD: This is how I will break the yoke of King Nebuchadnezzar of Babylon from the neck of all the nations within two years." (v. 11)

Jeremiah's response is curious. Freed from the yoke he was wearing, he just goes away. He does not respond to Hananiah, nor does he offer a proclamation to the people. He simply leaves (v. 11). But he will not remain distant from Hananiah for long. The story's narrator next reports that the word of the LORD comes to Jeremiah again and gives him a specific and clarifying message that must be delivered to Hananiah (v. 12).

The message Jeremiah delivers upstages Hananiah, points to his weakness as a prophet, and goes contrary to what Hananiah has previously proclaimed: the exile *will* happen. One last time Jeremiah confronts Hananiah, and this time he does not hold back anything. Jeremiah tells Hananiah to his face that the LORD has not sent him and that his words were a lie. Jeremiah's final proclamation to Hananiah has a bite to it: he announces that God is going to send him off the face of the earth, and that he will die within the year because by his words he has rebelled against God (vv. 14-16). The narrator's final comment sheds light on both Jeremiah and Hananiah. What Jeremiah pronounced as Hananiah's end does, indeed, happen; he dies. Thus Jeremiah shines as a true and faithful prophet, able to hold his own, open to the views and words of others, but discerning and discriminating at the same time.

Throughout the narrative Jeremiah develops as a character. His strong, clear voice and the manner in which he conducts himself furnish a model of self-confidence and an example of how to be self-possessed. His tact at conflict management is insightful. Sometimes he responds; at other times he just walks away. Most significant, however, is the fact that he, not Hananiah, has the last word, and it is this last word that crowns him "a true prophet" in the midst of his own. What Jeremiah had predicted does indeed happen. As for Hananiah, had he not "interfaced" with Jeremiah he might have survived. Both characters are a good match for each other, and both reveal, for audiences past and present, the challenges and spirit of the prophetic tradition as it tries to appropriate "the signs of the times."

Jeremiah 35:1-19: Jeremiah Encounters the Rechabites

The central theme of this narrative, featuring the Rechabites and the Judeans, is fidelity. The Rechabites act as a foil for the Judeans; they are faithful and listen to the command of their ancestor, Jonadab. The Judeans, for the most part, are not faithful; they have not listened to the command of their God. This narrative can be divided into three parts: (1) the Rechabites tested at the Temple (vv. 1-11), (2) a proclamation underscoring the Judeans' infidelity (vv. 12-17), and (3) a proclamation of promise to the Rechabites (vv. 18-19).

The narrator opens the first part of the narrative with a full description of what God says, on this occasion, to Jeremiah. The prophet is commanded by God to offer the Rechabites a test to see if they will remain faithful to the teachings of their ancestor, Jonadab. The test involves Jeremiah offering the Rechabites some wine, which they refuse because Jonadab, son of Rechab, had commanded them not to drink wine. Verses 1-11 picture Jeremiah meticulously carrying out God's directives, step by step, in "testing" the Rechabites, a test they pass. Jeremiah's audience learns that these people live in tents and own no vineyard, field, or seed. Moving away from the invading Babylonians who "came up against the land" (v. 11), the Rechabites eventually settled in Jerusalem with the Judeans.

Having sketched a portrait of the Rechabites, the narrator next focuses on Jeremiah and the people of Judah. Jeremiah is seen delivering God's word to the Judeans. Through the prophet God asks a simple rhetorical question that discloses the people's stubbornness and infidelity: "Can you not learn a lesson and obey my words?" God then expounds on the efforts made to draw Judah back to covenant relationship. The people not only rejected God, but also rejected the prophets God sent. The key word in the unit is "persistently." God, through the prophets, has spoken to the people persistently but to no avail. The adverb of consequence, "therefore," that begins a divine judgment statement, comes now as no surprise. The people of Judah are going to receive their just deserts.

The last section begins with a coordinate conjunction, "but," which the narrator uses to shift the audience's focus back to the Rechabites who, unlike the Judeans, live under God's promise (vv. 18-19).

The narrative functions as an instruction to the Judeans, holding up their portrait next to that of the Rechabites and allowing both Jeremiah and his mixed audience to see that there is no comparison. By testing and conversing with the Rechabites, Jeremiah has brought out the best in them. They live under promise as the Judeans live under terror. The narrator, Jeremiah, and God all see Judah as deserving of the consequences about to befall the Southern Kingdom. The narrative also points up how God can use nonbelievers to teach believers a powerful lesson. Finally, God's and Jeremiah's interaction with each other and with the community indicates the kind of fidelity God and Jeremiah enjoy with one another, a fidelity the community once had, but eventually lost.

Jeremiah 38:14-28: Jeremiah Encounters Zedekiah

One of the roles of the prophet is to act as an advisor to the king. Not all prophets in ancient Israel performed this duty, but some did. Jeremiah has had various encounters with King Zedekiah (see, e.g., Jer 37:1-10). In this passage Zedekiah "sends for" Jeremiah. Both king and prophet interface with one another in a lively exchange that provides Zedekiah with some hopeful directives in face of an approaching invasion. The entire passage is a dialogue between Zedekiah and Jeremiah. The narrative falls into three sections: verses 14-16, 17-23, and 24-28.

The first part of the narrative indicates that Zedekiah sent for Jeremiah so that he might consult with him. Here the narrator portrays the prophet as an assertive and savvy person who stakes out his own claims before he delivers God's harsh word of judgment to the king. Jeremiah is a clever negotiator who persuades Zedekiah to swear a secret oath that guarantees Jeremiah his life (vv. 14-16).

The second part of the narrative features Jeremiah delivering God's word to Zedekiah. The message is twofold: to surrender to the Babylonians would mean life; to resist them would mean death (vv. 17-18). Then, very candidly, King Zedekiah shares his feelings with Jeremiah: he is afraid of what the Babylonians might do to him. Here the narrator provides readers and hearers with a glimpse into the heart of a powerful leader: "I am afraid of the Judeans who have deserted to the Chaldeans, for I might be handed over to them and they would abuse me" (v. 19). Jeremiah's response to Zedekiah's fear is assertive, definitive, and bolstering: "This will not happen" (v. 20a). The certitude he offers Zedekiah, however, is contingent on the king's obedience to God as revealed to him through Jeremiah (v. 20b). What Jeremiah wants Zedekiah to do, ultimately, is surrender to the Babylonians, allow himself to be taken into exile, and thus have his life spared (Jer 34:1-7; cf. Jer 52:10-11).

Jeremiah then presents Zedekiah with another scenario (vv. 21-23). If he does not surrender, his wives and children will suffer, he will be seized by the Babylonians, and Jerusalem will be burned. Jeremiah tries to persuade Zedekiah to realize the seriousness of the message by telling him that it is part of a vision God gave him. The poem he sings to Zedekiah in the midst of their dialogue is another rhetorical device the prophet uses to underscore the magnitude of his warning. Robert P. Carroll draws out the symbolic relationship between the seizing of the women and children and the destruction of the city, and also offers a comment on the extended function of the poem:

> The harem will go to the victorious army, as is the inevitable fate of women in war: rape, concubinage, abuse and exploitation. Their treatment symbolizes the defeat of the kingdom, as does the leading out of

the royal sons to their captors. . . . Pathos is added to this picture of
the fall of Jerusalem by the placing of the brief poem in v. 22b in the
mouths of the women as they are led out to endure the lot of women
whenever men gain complete power over them. They mock Zedekiah
with a conventional poetic outcry, castigating him for his deception by
his companions and sneering at his plight.[4]

Jeremiah has given counsel to Zedekiah but, as history reveals, the king does
not heed the prophet's wise words.

Having heard the two possible scenarios, Zedekiah now responds to
Jeremiah. He offers no comment on what Jeremiah has said to him specifically. Instead, he swears Jeremiah to secrecy and tells him what he is to say
to the officials should they ask him what he said to the king. It is clear that
Zedekiah does not want his officials to know what the two possible scenarios
are. We are given to wonder, "why not?" Zedekiah's strategy discloses his
dilemma: his officials are determined to defend Jerusalem, and if he calls
for surrender he must face the wrath of officials and people both inside and
outside the city. He is in a no-win situation, and his instruction to Jeremiah
symbolizes his indecisiveness in this impasse.

Jeremiah is then questioned by the king's officials, and he replies to
them exactly as the king had requested. His staged answer quiets the inter-
rogation, and the narrator's final statement both tells the outcome of the
situation for Jeremiah and foreshadows future events: "And Jeremiah
remained in the court of the guard until the day that Jerusalem was taken"
(v. 28).

The exchange between Jeremiah and Zedekiah depicts Jeremiah fulfilling his role as a prophet: he gives advice to leaders, he tries to present a
reading of the "signs of the times," and he faithfully delivers God's word in
a way that is clear, creative, and wise. He presents two scenarios to the king
and leaves him free to decide what his choice will be. Jeremiah neither
coerces nor challenges; he merely advises. His tact in handling leadership
comes through in his exchange with the king's officials. By acceding to the
king's request about what he should say, Jeremiah does not add any more
fuel to a fire that is already beginning to burn out of control. Furthermore,
by complying with the king's wishes he allows the king to make the necessary maneuvers that will insure the fulfillment of the royal oath, namely,
that Zedekiah would not hand him over to those seeking his life. Thus we
see Jeremiah as politically astute, a posture that keeps him free to be able

---

[4] Robert P. Carroll, *Jeremiah.* OTL (Philadelphia: Westminster, 1986) 687.

to continue his mission. As for Zedekiah, he has his hands full. He is caught between the Babylonians and his own people. Eventually he will have to make a decision, and either way it is going to cost him his pride or his life.

Jeremiah 42:1-22: Pray to the LORD Your God for Us

Perhaps one of the most honest and poignant dialogues in the book of Jeremiah—comparable to the prophet's exchanges with his God—is the one between Jeremiah and members of his community who consult with him, begging him to pray to God on their behalf that they may receive a divine word through the prophet to provide direction for their lives. Jeremiah 42:1-22 is a tightly woven narrative that advances by means of a dialogue between Jeremiah and the people. The main characters are Jeremiah and a remnant who are left in Judah at Mizpah. The tension within the story includes this remnant's desire to go to Egypt, a choice neither Jeremiah nor God supports. The drama of the narrative unfolds in two parts: (1) the people's request for Jeremiah's divinely informed advice (vv. 1-6), and (2) Jeremiah's long proclamation, offering this remnant divinely inspired guidance (vv. 7-22). The climax comes in the last two verses.

The narrative opens with the remnant and their military leaders approaching Jeremiah with a special request. After acknowledging that they are few in number they entreat Jeremiah to pray for them so that they may receive divine guidance. Significant here is the remnant's recognition of Jeremiah as a man of prayer. Their comment: "Let the LORD your God show us where we should go and what we should do" (v. 3) indicates the confidence they have that Jeremiah's God will answer him and give him a word that will help them. How the remnant refers to God is curious. Three times they say "the LORD your God" (vv. 2, 3, 5). Is not Jeremiah's God their God too, or is such language suggestive of their distance from God?

Jeremiah responds affirmatively to the people's plea, and instead of referring to "the LORD my God" as we might expect, he says, "I am going to pray to the LORD your God as your request" (v. 4). Jeremiah's phrase clarifies for the remnant that God is not only his God but also their God. The people allude to this in their next response to Jeremiah, when they twice refer to God as "the LORD our God" and pledge their obedience to this God. Here the people are perceived as acting in earnest, but what needs to be remembered is their social situation: they are in Judah amidst the Babylonians; they are small in number and probably afraid; they are not sure what is in store for them, and so they cry out to God in their need and try to forge a relationship with God because of need and not because of love; for some, perhaps, it might be out of need *and* love.

The next half of the narrative features Jeremiah emerging, presumably from prayer, with a divine word for the remnant. He summons the people's military leaders together with the people themselves, and delivers a series of proclamations (vv. 7-22).[5] The first of these offers the people, in quick succession, a hope and a warning (vv. 9-12 and vv. 13-17, respectively). The shift in tone and focus is signaled by the word "but." Both proclamations are conditioned by the apodosis beginning with "if" (see v. 10 and v. 13) and the prodosis beginning with "then" (see v. 10 and v. 15).

The first proclamation provides a glimpse into God's divine plan and offers the people words of encouragement to strengthen them. God promises that if they remain in the land, God will build them up and not pull them down; God will plant them and not pluck them up (v. 10). The imagery here echoes the language of Jeremiah's call narrative (Jer 1:10). God's intention is to reestablish the people in the land. The presence of the remnant in the land now would be a symbol of what God hopes to do—create new life out of ruins and devastation. Both the people and the land will be restored to each other, and to God as well. Following the promise, God admits some strong, contrite feelings. God will bring about a change of events because God now has remorse: "I am sorry for the disaster that I have brought upon you" (v. 10). Such contrition is expressed to the remnant even though there has been no remorse on their part with regard to the people's apostasy and idolatrous ways. God is the first to reach out to offer reconciliation. God's promise to be with the people and to save them and rescue them from the hand of the Babylonian king is reminiscent of the promise God made to Jeremiah during his commissioning (see Jer 1:10). A final promise of mercy is heard in verse 12—mercy from God and from the king of Babylon. The remnant have been the recipients of Jeremiah's and God's tender, hope-filled, and grace-filled words. There is, however, another side. If the people insist on going to Egypt and following their own way instead of trusting in God's advice, they will suffer and die (vv. 15b-17). What is evident from Jeremiah's proclamation is that Israel's God is a God of promise, humility, and mercy who wants life, not death, for the people if only they will trust in God and follow God's advice instead of their own fear-ridden desires.

Although a positive image of God has been projected by Jeremiah and the text, the profile of God is still not without its problems. If the people are

---

[5] For a detailed analysis of these proclamations and their theological implications and claims see Walter Brueggemann, *Jeremiah: Exile and Homecoming* (Grand Rapids: Eerdmans, 1998) 390–93.

not obedient to God, and if they do follow their own ways, then, according to Jeremiah and the text, God will punish them severely. Although such an attitude reflects the theology and culture of the day, could not the warning be a polemic against the power of the king of Babylon? Which would be more difficult for the people to endure—the suffering inflicted by the king or the suffering inflicted by God, who is mightier than any power on earth? God's warning may contain a subtle note of persuasion. It remains, however, inherently violent.

The third proclamation in this second section of the narrative picks up the theme introduced in the second proclamation. Here God spells out to the remnant what will happen if they do not heed the divine advice (v. 18). Then, without any markers to indicate a shift in speakers, Jeremiah recounts for the remnant what he has done on their behalf. In the final two verses he undoubtedly takes the people by surprise because, after having been so compliant to their wishes, he now tells them exactly what he thinks about them and where they stand:

> So I have told you today, but you have not obeyed the voice of the LORD your God in anything that he sent me to tell you. (v. 21)

Jeremiah has called their hand, showing them that he suspects or even knows their opinion of him and their recalcitrant attitude and stubbornness toward their God. He issues them a final warning (v. 22), and ultimately lets them decide for themselves what their fate will be, depending on the choice they themselves will make. Jeremiah no longer shouts out, performs symbolic actions, or tries to coerce the people with imaginative proclamations. He merely delivers God's word, advises, and steps back to let his listeners choose. He is a person self-possessed, wise, and free.

In Retrospect . . .

Jeremiah as God's prophet interacts with many different kinds of people. It is through these interactions that one sees the steady development of his character, the deepening commitment he has to his mission and the living out of it, and his willingness to engage in conversation not only with the common folk but also with those in significant leadership positions. He goes to whom God sends him, speaks whatever God declares to him, and willingly embraces the risks associated with his tasks. Remaining faithful to God and to his mission, he continues to be a sign of hope, a beacon of light even in the most unsettled of times. Preacher of grace, poet of truth, distiller of wisdom, Jeremiah is a figure who confronts, disturbs, unsettles. Politically astute and unassumingly wise, he is the people's greatest hope for life if only they will listen and heed his words.

CHAPTER SIX

The One Who Prays . . .

Introduction

From earliest biblical times those entrusted with the gift of leadership have been women and men of prayer. Moses prayed to God on behalf of the Israelites when they angered their God by making a golden calf (Exod 32:7-14; 33:12-23); David talked to God about the promise he received concerning his house (2 Sam 7:1-29); Solomon prayed to God for wisdom in governing the great nation he inherited from his father David (1 Kgs 3:3-15); Judith prayed on behalf of her people who were being overpowered by the Assyrians (Judith 9).[1] Jeremiah is no different from his ancestors in this regard; he, too, is a person of prayer and, like Moses, tries to intercede on behalf of his people—a people who have been unfaithful to God like so many of their ancestors before them. God, however, pained and angered by the infidelity and transgressions of Israel—a people God loves so much—does not even want to hear Jeremiah intercede on their behalf. Yet Jeremiah will pray to his God on behalf of his people because, like God, he cannot forsake them. The skillful use of rhetoric in each passage draws out the character of Jeremiah while drawing Jeremiah's audience into the drama of his relationship with his God.

Jeremiah 7:16-20: Do Not Pray . . .

Completely disgusted with the people's apostasy, idolatry, and general baseness, God informs Jeremiah that he is not to intercede for this wayward

---

[1] See also Num 11:2; 14:11-24; 16:20-50; Deut 9:13-29; 10:10; 1 Sam 7:5-11; 12:17-18; 15:11.

people.[2] In this narrative, which is part of a larger judgment proclamation against Judah (Jer 7:1–9:26), God is the main speaker, addressing Jeremiah very personally and being reported by a narrator: "The word that came to Jeremiah from the LORD . . ." (7:1).

God's personal address begins with a *casus pendens,* "as for you," followed by three imperatives that instruct Jeremiah not to pray on behalf of the people: "do not pray for this people, do not raise a cry or prayer on their behalf, and do not intercede with me, for I will not hear you" (v. 16). The triple imperative makes God's wishes perfectly clear to Jeremiah, while stressing emphatic divine displeasure with the people. The irony inherent in the statement is that God, in fact, is hearing Jeremiah. The implication is that God will not "listen" to Jeremiah and follow Jeremiah's wishes. Verses 17-19 are a double proclamation against the people, one directed to Jeremiah (vv. 17-18) and the other directed against the people (v. 19).

Verse 17 opens with a rhetorical question: "Do you not see what they are doing in the towns of Judah and in the streets of Jerusalem?" that suggests the people's depravity and points out to Jeremiah why he should not pray for the people. "In the towns of Judah and in the streets of Jerusalem" is a stock phrase that here emphasizes the extent of idolatry: it is widespread throughout the Southern Kingdom, even in Jerusalem, God's "holy city." The disloyalty hinted at in verse 17 is described fully in verse 18:

> The children gather wood, the fathers kindle fire, and the women knead dough, to make cakes for the queen of heaven; and they pour out drink offerings to other gods, to provoke me to anger.

Here God directly informs Jeremiah that idolatry has become a "family affair." And those people of Jeremiah's day who are listening to the prophet's proclamations hear indirectly about the religious depravity that has God wild with rage. "The queen of heaven" may be a metaphorical description of Ishtar, a goddess associated with "love, sexuality, and war."[3] Surprisingly,

---

[2] Intercessory prayer was one of the primary tasks of the prophetic vocation. For further discussion of the prophets as intercessors see Samuel E. Balentine, "The Prophet as Intercessor: A Reassessment," *JBL* 103 (1984) 161–73; and Arnold B. Rhodes, "Israel's Prophets as Intercessors," in Arthur L. Merrill and Thomas W. Overholt, eds., *Scripture in History and Theology: Essays in Honor of J. Coert Rylaarsdam* (Pittsburgh: Pickwick Press, 1988) 107–28.

[3] See Jack R. Lundbom, *Jeremiah 1–20.* AB 21A (New York: Doubleday, 1999) 476–77, for a detailed discussion of the "queen of heaven," with cross listings of additional bibliographic material for further study.

Israel's God seems to have some features similar to those of this astral deity.

Verse 19 features a double rhetorical question that God intends for the idolatrous people, even though the questions are posed to Jeremiah in the course of God's conversation with him: "'Is it I whom they provoke?' says the LORD. "Is it not themselves, to their own hurt?" The inference here is that by their idolatry the people have indicted themselves. And the irony of the first question is that they have indeed provoked God (see v. 18). Thus the question turns on the preceding statement made by God, with "provoke" as a keyword used to create narrative coherence and contrast.

Picking up on the irony of verses 18-19, God, having been "provoked," now issues a word of judgment not only against the idolatrous people but also against the animals, the trees, and the fruit of the ground (v. 20). God's judgment encompasses both the human and the non-human world. This description, with the ominous conclusion "it will burn and not be quenched," indicates just how provoked God truly is, and foreshadows the horrible effects the impending battle in Judah will have when Jerusalem is burned, the Temple is destroyed, and the land, its animals, and the people are all ravaged by military invasion. God's wrath will not be quenched; there is to be nothing left of the Southern Kingdom.

Now that Jeremiah has heard, once again, God's intentions for this unfaithful people, such an order not to pray for the people would undoubtedly have left the prophet feeling helpless and melancholic. The inevitable was going to happen; God had made up God's mind, and Jeremiah was not going to be able to do a thing to stop it. The only thing he could do was to continue to make known God's pain and anger and impending wrath, hoping that the people would hear him, acknowledge their sins, and return to God. God is holding the people responsible for their offenses and no one is going to move God to compassion until justice is served.

One final point: for today's readers and hearers of this text it is important to note again that the character Jeremiah, along with the author and editors of the book of Jeremiah, is reading and interpreting historical events through a theological lens colored by the deuteronomistic theology of retribution.

Jeremiah 11:14-17: Do Not Pray . . .

This passage begins with the same *casus pendens* heard in 7:16, "as for you," followed by a command also similar to that in 7:16. Jeremiah is told again not to pray for "this people" or lift up a cry or prayer on their behalf because God will not listen, and this time it is not Jeremiah who will not be heard, but the people who would call on God in their time of trouble

(v. 14). This narrative, like Jeremiah 7:16-20, features God speaking to Jeremiah in the same manner, with the same tone, and on the same theme, but now the images and message are more intimate and addressed directly to the apostate people. The third-person pronouns found in 7:16-20 have become second-person pronouns in 11:14-17. Also similar to 7:16-20 is the use of three successive rhetorical questions:

> What right has my beloved in my house, when she has done vile deeds?
> Can vows and sacrificial flesh avert your doom? Can you then exult?
> (v. 15)

Here God questions the people's right to be in the Temple, because of their vile deeds, and makes the point that promises and offerings cannot stop what is about to befall them. There is no room for celebration; the text implies that this is a time for contrition after acknowledgment of one's offense. The community is depicted in female metaphorical language appropriate to covenant, but such language reinforces certain female stereotypes.

In verses 16-17 the tone shifts again. The God who once talked personally to the people now assumes some distance, indicated not by a change in pronoun references but rather by God's referring to God's self in the third person: "What right has my beloved in my house, when she has done vile deeds? Can vows and sacrificial flesh avert your doom? Can you then exult?" God has stepped back from the relationship with the people as the people have stepped out of relationship with God. In verse 16a God reminisces about how the people were once called "a green olive tree, fair with goodly fruit." The metaphor, derived from the people's agrarian social location, speaks of a certain lushness and vitality. Olive trees were a staple in Israel's subsistence and commercial economy. This splendid image shifts in verses 16b-17 as God foreshadows what is going to happen to the olive tree, and ultimately to the house of Israel and the house of Judah, because of their idolatry. God is going to set the olive tree ablaze, and it will burn up. So shall Israel and Judah be destroyed. War images lurk in the background, accented by the metaphor, "LORD of hosts," a reference to the warrior God. The image of God "planting" the people envisions God as a gardener (cf. Isaiah 5). What God has planted, God is now going to uproot (cf. Jer 1:10). Because Israel and Judah have sacrificed to Baal, the chief fertility god, this people—this beautiful olive tree that once bore goodly fruit—will now be destroyed. Once again Jeremiah's intercession cannot stop the inevitable. God's appeal to the people's hearts and imaginations is all for naught. This hypocritical people now stands judged by a resolute God.

Jeremiah 14:11-12: Do not Pray . . .

Varying the theme, Jeremiah again reports what God has said to him about interceding for the people:

> Do not pray for the welfare of this people. Although they fast, I do not hear their cry, and although they offer burnt offering and grain offering, I do not accept them; but by the sword, by famine, and by pestilence I consume them. (vv. 11-12)

The people's offerings will not alter God's decision to bring judgment upon them (Jer 11:15), and their expressions of mourning and atonement will not cause God to have a change of heart. By refusing to acknowledge their offenses they are bringing inevitable suffering on themselves, and to be faithful to God's word, the prophet must remain silent toward God.

Jeremiah 14:17-22: A Poet Prays . . .

Jeremiah is forbidden to pray for the people, but now God tells him to sing a lament on the people's behalf. God gives Jeremiah the words—"You shall say to them this word"— expressing God's pathos, and essentially Jeremiah's as well.[4] As Walter Brueggemann observes, "the pathos of the poet, in this poetry, is presented as the pathos of God." Thus begins Jeremiah's lament in the words of God:

> Let my eyes run down with tears night and day,
> and let them not cease. . . . (v. 17a)

Verses 17-18 are a description of Judah's fate. Jeremiah laments the devastation of the Southern Kingdom caused by the sword and famine. The people have been struck down by a double blow—". . . the virgin daughter —my people—is struck down with a crushing blow, with a very grievous wound" (v. 17b). The metaphor presents God as a father and Judah, in a feminine *persona,* as "my people." The possessive pronoun suggests rela-

---

[4] Lundbom agrees that YHWH is not the speaker of vv. 17-22 (see ibid.), but Walter Brueggemann disagrees and comments that "it is as though the prophet is mandated by God to articulate the lament" (*A Commentary on Jeremiah: Exile and Homecoming* [Grand Rapids: Eerdmans, 1998] 138–39). On the basis of the overall movement and storyline of the book, I concur with Brueggemann, contra Lundbom.

tionship between God and the people, and between Jeremiah and the people. From the content of this lament it is clear that neither God nor Jeremiah has abandoned the people even in their miserable state. The "very grievous wound" is metaphorical and refers to God's chastisement, one that causes as much pain to God as it does to the people. Jeremiah laments the loss of spiritual vision among the people:

> For both prophet and priest ply their trade throughout the land,
>   and have no knowledge. (v. 18c)

Verse 19 is an address to God. Here Jeremiah imagines the people confronting God with three direct rhetorical questions that express pain, frustration, and bewilderment. It is clear that the people still do not understand how they have offended God:

> Why have you struck us down
>   so that there is no healing for us?

The question foreshadows the total devastation of Judah. The people will have no peace and no healing, only terror. Jeremiah foreshadows what they are going to experience emotionally, and laments it. Finally, in verse 20, comes the breakthrough. God, through Jeremiah, envisions the people acknowledging their offense:

> We acknowledge our wickedness, O LORD,
>   the iniquity of our ancestors,
>   for we have sinned against you.

But what is their wickedness, and how have they sinned against their God? The people's confession is only partial. Thus some will die by the sword and famine, and some will be spared.

Verse 21 is a plea. Here God, through Jeremiah, imagines the people making a very clever appeal to God, begging God not to disdain them for the sake of God's own reputation. The request, "remember and do not break your covenant with us," is ironic! God has kept covenant, but the people have not.

Verse 22 is also a confession. Here God, through Jeremiah, envisions the people addressing God and indirectly acknowledging God as greater than any of the idols, as the two rhetorical questions point out, all of which culminates in the final question. Here the people finally acknowledge their

God to be greater than Baal, the fertility god they have been worshiping. This reference to Baal is suggested in the imagery of the first two rhetorical questions:

> Can any idols of the nations bring rain?
>   Or can the heavens give showers?
> Is it not you, O LORD our God?

The phrase "our God" suggests that the people are once more claiming God as their own, the God in whom they now hope, but only because they see the devastation that has happened to them (cf. vv. 17-18)—and this is only the beginning. Will God hear them, and will their fate be altered? God and Jeremiah hint otherwise (see Jeremiah 15).

Jeremiah 16:19-21: A Prayer for Trust

> O LORD, my strength and my stronghold,
>   my refuge in the day of trouble,
> to you shall the nations come
>   from the ends of the earth and say:
> Our ancestors have inherited nothing but lies,
>   worthless things in which there is no profit.
> Can mortals make for themselves gods?
>   Such are no gods! (vv. 19-20)

What a wonderful prayer Jeremiah has spoken to God, and what a magnificent vision of unity he has offered his hearers and readers! Jeremiah opens his poetic prayer with a personal acknowledgment of who God is in his life, followed by a picture of universal oneness—all nations coming to Israel's God and acknowledging that all other gods are worthless.

Does such a prayer preclude the impending disaster? No: the nations, including Israel, will come to understand that there is only one God in whom all power rests, but only when the catastrophic worldwide military battles ensue and Babylon is defeated once and for all. When the nations are "leveled," with no help from their gods, then their experience will show them Israel's God as the one true God (see Jer 16:21). The historical events this prayer indirectly foreshadows can only leave one aghast. Contemporary readers and listeners eavesdropping on Jeremiah at prayer need to take consolation in realizing, once again, how the theology and history of the times underlie the contents of Jeremiah's poem to his God. Finally, as in the prayer in Jeremiah 14:17-22, God speaks through Jeremiah, and those who hear him receive an insight into what will transpire after disaster strikes: namely, world conversion. Today this aspect of the prophet's prayer remains eschatological in the midst of repeating history.

Jeremiah 32:16-25: Help Me to Understand . . .

Of all the prayers Jeremiah prays, perhaps this one in 32:16-25 is the most poignant, because he himself speaks to God directly and asks for understanding. Seeing the horror that he has been announcing beginning to happen, and having bought a piece of land in Judah as God had directed him to do in the midst of the Babylonians' advance, Jeremiah stands bewildered by his own actions. Thus, in narrative form, he tells his audience(s) the story of how he approached God to have a good talk about his personal confusion. His recounting of the conversation begins in verse 16 with an editorial comment linking the previous pericope, 32:1-15, to the present one and showing Jeremiah to be a wonderful storyteller who is conscious of his audience as he tries to piece together and narrate the events of his own life in relation to the world and the people around him. Hence he opens his prayer with a temporal clause: "After I had given the deed of purchase to Baruch son of Neriah, I prayed to the LORD, saying . . ." (v. 16). Verses 17-25 disclose the contents of Jeremiah's prayer.

In his prayer Jeremiah first acknowledges God as LORD of creation (vv. 16-19). Embedded in this hymn of praise are images suggestive of the Exodus tradition. For example, "your outstretched arm" is a stock phrase that personifies God's strength. It alludes to Exodus 6:6, where it first appears in the Old Testament: this, God tells Moses, is how the Israelites will be freed from Egyptian bondage. Jeremiah is recalling the history of his ancestors, which has shaped his life and the life of his community thus far, and he acknowledges God's presence in shaping that past as he proclaims, "Nothing is too hard for you" (v. 17).

Next Jeremiah acknowledges God's great and enduring love, but also God's justice: "You show steadfast love to the thousandth generation, but repay the guilt of parents into the laps of their children after them" (v. 18). This too is an allusion to the Exodus tradition (see Exod 34:7), with undertones of the deuteronomistic theology of retribution. Jeremiah has seen and experienced both God's steadfast love and the repayment of the guilt of the ancestors into the laps of the children (cf. Jer 2:1–4:4); the Northern Kingdom of Israel has fallen and Judah is about to fall.

"The LORD of hosts" is another stock phrase that identifies God as a warrior god. Jeremiah recognizes this God of hosts as one who sees people's ways and rewards them accordingly. The inherent irony is that Jeremiah also sees the people's ways—how unfaithful and corrupt they have become. They have borne bad fruit, and thus they have determined their own divine "reward," which is not going to be gratuitous. Jeremiah knows that God's outstretched arm is not going to be for the salvation of Israel as it was in the days of the Exodus; rather, it will be for judgment—a mighty judgment as in the days of the prophet Amos (see Amos 1–2; cf. Ezek 20:33, 34).

In verses 20-23 Jeremiah rehearses Israel's deliverance from Egypt and in doing so highlights God's goodness and the name God has made for God's self, one that has endured to the present moment—LORD of hosts (see v. 18). By referring again to God's "outstretched arm," now in conjunction with God's strong hand, Jeremiah emphasizes an earlier point made about God's might (see v. 17). God freed Israel from oppression not only with a strong hand and an outstretched arm but also "with great terror" (v. 21). The Egyptians fled from the Israelites (Exod 14:25). It was only after these mighty deeds that the people believed in the God of Israel (cf. Jer 16:19-21). Jeremiah knows that God's terror will come upon people again as in the days of old, but this time it will be on the people of Judah, a reversal of history for the Israelites that will take them by surprise (see Jer 20:10). The land given to them through inheritance from their ancestors, which Jeremiah alludes to next, will, ironically, be taken away from them. The people, as Jeremiah foresees, are about to be plucked up, their king, Zedekiah, pulled down from the throne and taken into captivity, and Jerusalem and the kingdom destroyed (cf. Jer 1:10). This time the people of Judah will be running away from the enemy instead of the enemy running away from Israel (see Jer 39:1-10). The land the Israelites once took as their own possession will be lost to the Babylonians, who will march in and take possession.

With the content of his prayer set against the present unfolding reality, it would seem that Jeremiah is hoping to awaken his audience to the reality of who God is and has been throughout Israel's history, alerting them to certain contrasts and reversals disguised in familiar images and metaphors. History is changing for God's people but, even with Jeremiah's imaginative strategies to help them see, the people are unable to perceive the grave events that are about to take place. His prayer boldly and openly indicts them once more, signaled by the word "but":

> But they did not obey your voice or follow your law; of all you commanded them to do, they did nothing. (v. 23)

Jeremiah, in his prayer, is "making the connections"; if only his people would do the same!

The next phrase, "therefore you have made all these disasters come upon them," links the past with the present. The people are no different from their ancestors; disasters have already befallen them in the Assyrian invasion and deportation, and disaster is about to strike them again with the Babylonian invasion and exile. Jeremiah steps forward into the present, impending reality:

> See, the siege-ramps have been cast up against the city to take it, and the city, faced with sword, famine, and pestilence, has been given into the hands of the Chaldeans who are fighting against it. What you spoke has happened, as you yourself can see. (v. 24)

Jeremiah the poet, the storyteller, the man of prayer has let his God know, as well as his listeners, that he is aware of what is happening. He has appealed to Israel's history, and by retelling it against the backdrop of the present has painted a marvelous picture of continuity with colors that contrast to shed new light on an otherwise familiar scene. Preacher of grace, poet of truth, painter of light—Jeremiah's prayer reveals him as a creative genius, and yet he is puzzled.

In verse 25 Jeremiah does not question God's past directive to him, which he did perform (see Jeremiah 32). He merely comments on it in wonderment and in light of all that he has confessed to knowing:

> Yet, you, O Lord GOD, have said to me, "Buy the field for money and get witnesses"—though the city has been given into the hands of the Chaldeans.

In the context of his historical reality Jeremiah sees what he did as inconsequential to present and future events as he perceives them. What he does not perceive at this point, however—until God reveals it to him (vv. 26-44)—is that God's ways are also paradoxical. Embedded in Jeremiah's action is a vision of hope for his people. A people in possession of land, given as gift, will become dispossessed of the land only to later repossess it, but this time they will have to buy it back through their own efforts, with God's grace.

In Retrospect . . .

All the texts examined in this chapter draw attention to Jeremiah as a person of prayer. Though he desires to fulfill his role as a prophet by interceding for his people in an attempt to avert God's anger and its consequences, he is told repeatedly not to pray for "this people." And he listens. He talks to God instead about all that he has known and seen. By doing so, he gives his people a great gift—a vision of God's intentions for them, and for other nations as well. Jeremiah cannot stop the inevitable; God will not let it be stopped. History will unfold; God will let it unfold; and human beings are not in a position to do anything about it because it is too late—they are too caught up. There will be an end, but this end will be the start of a new beginning. In their tragic state the best word Jeremiah can offer is not a word of intercession but a word of hope, performed through his life and the choices he makes. God's final word is not destruction and annihilation; it is restoration, resettlement, and reunion, all of which are foreshadowed in Jeremiah's prayers: reunion with God, reunion with one another, reunion in the land:

> See, today I appoint you over nations and over kingdoms,
>> to pluck up and to pull down,
>> to destroy and to overthrow,
>> to build and to plant. (Jer 1:10)

CHAPTER SEVEN

The Paradox of Letting Go

Introduction

Destined to see the downfall of his people, the burning of God's holy city Jerusalem, the destruction of the Temple, and the loss of land with eventual exile for its inhabitants, and struggling to be faithful to a God, a vocation, and a mission that has cost, is costing, and will cost him no less than everything, Jeremiah stands in the midst of peril and promise. Having seen so much already through the eyes of this poet-storyteller, we now wonder what he must have felt as he staggered under the burden of all God had entrusted to him and was asking of him. Perhaps no better insight can be gleaned than from the words of the character himself. Jeremiah's verbal expressions of struggle and pain, pathos and bafflement, intermittently mixed with moments of joy and glimmers of hope, are a window into his heart and ultimately into the heart of his God as well. Jeremiah, preacher of grace and poet of truth, the one rejected by many and understood by few, stands vulnerable, revealing for all time the wondrous mystery of the divine in the human.

Jeremiah 4:19-26: My Anguish, My Anguish

For the ancient Jewish people the heart was the central organ. It was the seat of all emotion, intelligence, intuition, and knowledge. The heart is where God dwells. For Jeremiah, the foreskin of whose heart was figuratively "circumcised" (Jer 4:4), the heart was where he felt all the pain of what he saw. Jeremiah 4:19-26 is a word from the prophet's heart:

My anguish, my anguish! I writhe in pain!
    Oh, the walls of my heart!
My heart is beating wildly;
    I cannot keep silent;
for I hear the sound of the trumpet,
    the alarm of war. (v. 19)

Jeremiah's honest cry reveals his own pain over what is to unfold. In verse 20 he depicts some of what he sees, and then poses a poignant rhetorical question that receives no answer from God or anyone else:

Disaster overtakes disaster,
    the whole land is laid waste.
Suddenly my tents are destroyed,
    my curtains in a moment.
How long must I see the standard,
    and hear the sound of the trumpet?

Jeremiah's painful cry foreshadows the events yet to occur. What is the word that Jeremiah cannot keep silent (v. 19)? It is God's word, which Jeremiah quotes in verse 22:

"For my people are foolish,
    they do not know me;
they are stupid children,
    they have no understanding.
They are skilled in doing evil,
    but do not know how to do good."

This time Jeremiah's people stand indicted for their lack of intelligence, coupled with their wicked deeds. The metaphor implies God as parent, with the Israelites as "stupid children," but how could they have any understanding and any knowledge of God when their hearts remain supposedly uncircumcised and unfaithful to their God (cf. Jer 4:4)? Jeremiah's contrasting images are disconcerting. One would expect the people to be skilled in doing good, but here just the opposite is true.

Verses 23-26 catalogue what Jeremiah sees: total devastation. What he hinted at in verse 20 now comes into full view. The repetition of "I looked," followed by description after description of disaster, confirms the giftedness of Jeremiah as a prophet who has seen all this in his mind's eye. Jeremiah attributes the horrible sight of impending judgment to God's fierce anger.

Again one must be mindful of the deuteronomistic theology of retribution that has colored the message and shaped this text. Walter Brueggemann notes that "the fourfold 'I looked' is a staggering study of creation run amok, creation reverted to chaos,"[1] a point that can be supported through the tabulation of parallels between Genesis 1 and these verses in Jeremiah:

Genesis 1	*Jeremiah 4:23-26*
CREATION	CHAOS
1:2: formless and void	4:23: waste and void
1:3: light	4:23: light
1:8: heavens	4:23: heavens
1:10: earth	4:23: earth
1:20: birds	4:25: birds
1:26: humankind	4:25: no person[2]

Is it any wonder, then, that Jeremiah's heart beats wildly as he writhes in pain? He knows that this cosmic vision of destruction will come to pass.

Jeremiah 6:10-11: I am Full of the Wrath of the LORD . . .

Having proclaimed God's word of judgment faithfully, and having hoped against hope that the people would hear, acknowledge their offenses, and thus return to God, Jeremiah vents his frustration:

> To whom shall I speak and give warning,
>   that they may hear?
> See, their ears are closed,
>   they cannot listen.
> The word of the LORD is to them
>   an object of scorn;
>   they take no pleasure in it.
> But I am full of the wrath of the LORD;
>   I am weary of holding it in. (vv. 10-11)

---

[1] Walter Brueggemann, *A Commentary on Jeremiah: Exile and Homecoming* (Grand Rapids: Eerdmans, 1998) 59.

[2] This chart is adapted from the one presented by Peter C. Craigie, Page H. Kelley, and Joel F. Drinkard, Jr., in their *Jeremiah 1–25*. WBC 26 (Dallas: Word Books, 1991) 81.

The rhetorical question and comment point up the futility of Jeremiah's mission because of the people's hard-heartedness, leading to their lack of receptivity to God's and the poet's word (cf. 4:4). Jeremiah notes the people's response to God's word: they mock it and do not delight in it. The inherent irony in this statement for Jeremiah is that he, as an embodiment of God's word, is also, and will continue to be, an object of scorn. Eventually he realizes and laments that fact as well (see Jer 20:10). Furthermore, who would not scorn God's word? And who would take pleasure in it? God's word is a harsh word: judgment and impending doom. But Jeremiah had hoped the people would take pleasure in it because when once a person or group of people know the truth about themselves or the group in general, and that sense of truth reveals those aspects still in need of healing and transformation, they have an opportunity to acknowledge the truth and work with it constructively. Preacher of grace, poet of truth—Jeremiah understands the opportunities God's word provides and he struggles with a people who do not.

In verse 11 Jeremiah acknowledges a feeling within himself that overwhelms him so that he longs to gush it out. He is filled with God's wrath. Is this "wrath of the LORD" metaphorical? Is Jeremiah saying that he is "filled with the wrath of the LORD" at the people's inability to hear and respond to the word he preaches? Or is he acknowledging that he now shares in God's wrath as the passion that energizes him and pushes him to proclaim the uncomfortable, disconcerting, and repulsive word he has been preaching all along concerning the people's fate and that of Jerusalem and Judah? Given his further comment, "I am weary of holding it in" (v. 11b), the latter seems more plausible. Thus Jeremiah has revealed the power, energy, and motivation behind his preaching: the spirit of God. Jeremiah embodies God's spirit made manifest through what he says and how he says it (cf. Jer 20:9). Although his own people may not recognize Jeremiah as God's gift to them, contemporary readers can see in Jeremiah the identity, growth, and development of a prophetic personality and a marvelous passion that can too often be misunderstood, judged inappropriately, and worse, stifled.

Jeremiah 8:18–9:3: My Heart is Sick . . .

Jeremiah as God's prophet feels not only God's pain but also his people's pain, which may go unexpressed until one like Jeremiah comes along and makes known the word that lies deepest within the heart of God and that of God's people. Jeremiah 8:18–9:3 is Jeremiah's lament over the coming judgment, which the poet sings as if that judgment is already occurring. Jeremiah himself grieves at his own experience while feeling his people's pain. The poet begins his lament with a very personal expression of his feelings that sets the tone for the entire passage:

> My joy is gone, grief is upon me,
> > my heart is sick. (v. 18)

Why has Jeremiah's joy gone? Why is grief upon him? Why is his heart sick? The answer follows in verses 19-21:

> Hark, the cry of my poor people
> > from far and wide in the land:
> "Is the LORD not in Zion?
> > Is her King not in her?"
> ("Why have they provoked me to anger with their images,
> > with their foreign idols?")
> "The harvest is past, the summer is ended,
> > and we are not saved."
> For the hurt of my poor people I am hurt,
> > I mourn, and dismay has taken hold of me.

Jeremiah's heart grieves, bereft of joy, because he hears the cry of his poor people, twice quoted. The first quotation is a rhetorical question that highlights God's absence from the holy city: "Is the LORD not in Zion? Is her King not in her?" (v. 19a). Indirectly the people are taking God to task for having abdicated the throne. The second quotation is a self-reflective comment in which the people reveal their own lamentable state: "The harvest is past, the summer is ended, and we are not saved" (v. 20). For these reasons Jeremiah mourns (v. 18a; cf. v. 21b). But why is Jeremiah's heart sick? The answer can be found in verse 19, where Jeremiah quotes God: "Why have they provoked me to anger with their images, with their foreign idols?" Jeremiah's heart mirrors the heart of his people. Their hearts are sick because they have been unfaithful to their God and their lives are threatened. Jeremiah's heart is sick because he feels God's pain over the people's infidelity, and also because he knows the people have provoked God and that divine judgment is just around the corner. Thus "dismay" also takes hold of him (v. 21). The phrase "my poor people" in verses 19 and 21 functions like an *inclusio* and helps to unify the passage, with its interlocking quotations and central message of lamentation.

Jeremiah next asks three rhetorical questions: (1) "Is there no balm in Gilead?" (2) "Is there no physician there?" and (3) "Why then has the health of my poor people not been restored?" Yes, there is balm in Gilead; yes, there is a physician there. But why haven't the people been restored to health? The answer is simple: ironically, even though there is balm and a physician in Gilead, the people's health cannot be restored through medicinal means; they can only be healed by their God, a healing that can only begin with their acknowledgment of their offense against God. In Jeremiah's third question lies a triple irony. He knows that there is a balm and a physician; he knows that only God can heal; he knows why the people's health has not been restored. This third rhetorical question, posed in the context of the other two, functions as an expression of Jeremiah's own feigned bewilderment to his people while at the same time he holds up a mirror to them, hoping that they will ask these same questions and enter into some sort of self-reflective process. The phrase "my poor people" echoes verses 19 and 21 and helps to create poetic unity while emphasizing Jeremiah's sentiment.

Following the three rhetorical questions, Jeremiah next expresses his feelings with two wish statements:

> O that my head were a spring of water,
>   and my eyes a fountain of tears,
> so that I might weep day and night
>   for the slain of my poor people!
> O that I had in the desert
>   a traveler's lodging place,
> that I might leave my people
>   and go away from them!
> For they are all adulterers,
>   a band of traitors. (9:1-2)

In the first wish statement Jeremiah expresses his lament metaphorically. He wishes his head could be a "spring" and a "fountain" so that he could weep unceasingly for the slain of his "poor people." Here he foresees their tragic fate and speaks as if it has already happened. In the second wish statement he expresses a sentiment different from the first. Now he wants to run away from his people because they are so corrupt. He sees them as "adulterers" and "a band of traitors." Jeremiah has openly indicted his own people and stated publicly what he personally thinks about them. He wants no part of their wickedness and longs to be far away from them. The irony is that he, like God, remains with them to the bitter end of the fall of Jerusalem and the Southern Kingdom and on into exile. The use of the personal pronoun "my" with the word "people" is significant. Jeremiah identifies the people as his own and stands among them, but he is not one with them in their choices. Finally, the phrase "my poor people," used again in 9:1, joins this unit (9:1-2) to 8:22 and 8:18-21, helping to create a sense of repetitive use of the phrase in 8:18–9:2 (4x) that emphasizes the condition of the community and how Jeremiah, ultimately, looks on them: He pities them.

One further hermeneutical point: are all the people adulterers and a band of traitors within the community, as Jeremiah claims? Or is he looking at the community corporately without mentioning those few individuals who may have remained faithful to God? Viewing a group corporately, as well as the notion of "corporate punishment" whereby all are threatened with divine chastisement because of the offenses of a few, was a popular stance in the ancient world. There are remnants of this attitude today, and it calls for ongoing assessment in light of our changing notions of justice.

Jeremiah 10:19-20: Woe is Me . . .

Part of a larger unit that speaks of the coming exile (Jer 10:17-25), verses 19-20 focus on the unexpressed pain of the community that Jeremiah so poignantly voices from within:

> Woe is me because of my hurt!
>> My wound is severe.
> But I said, "Truly this is my punishment,
>> and I must bear it."
> My tent is destroyed,
>> and all my cords are broken;
> my children have gone from me,
>> and they are no more;
> there is no one to spread my tent again,
>> and to set up my curtains.

Jeremiah feels the pain of the blow yet to be struck: the Babylonian invasion and destruction of the Temple, the Southern Kingdom, and Jerusalem. He laments as if this wound has already happened and the people have already been exiled. In the first line of the lament Jeremiah gives voice to the community, pining its painful experience (v. 19a). In the second line he speaks in his own voice, signaled by the phrase "but I said," which begins his own lament and what, perhaps, he would wish the community to say but instead states on their behalf (v. 19b). In v. 20 he sings again in the voice of the community. Although one hears the community's pain through Jeremiah, one hears only from the prophet himself that the punishment is deserved. "Woe is me because of my heart!" Jeremiah's lament suggests a sense of self-pity on the part of the community. In this regard Jeremiah's own voice in verse 19b serves as a response to the community's voice heard through Jeremiah in verses 19a and 20.

Jeremiah 10:23-25: Correct Me, O LORD . . .

The poet's lament continues in Jeremiah 10:23-25. In a reflective prayer Jeremiah has a heart-to-heart conversation with God. While this prayer is deeply personal, it is also intercessory. In verse 23 Jeremiah acknowledges the limitations of human beings:

> I know, O LORD, that the way of human beings is not in their control,
>   that mortals as they walk cannot direct their steps.

Humanity is not in control of its own direction; there are other forces guiding it, though they are not named. Verses 24-25 contain a request for justice. First Jeremiah asks that he be rightly chastised, presumably for his own offenses, and he begs God that this correction not be done in anger. Jeremiah acknowledges that divine anger can be lethal.

> Correct me, O LORD, but in just measure;
>   not in your anger, or you will bring me to nothing.

Behind Jeremiah's own voice is the prophet speaking on behalf of the community, interceding for them not by asking God simply to forget about the people's offenses, but praying that God will chastise them fairly. The irony is that God does "correct" the people with anger, and they are brought to nothing. The Southern Kingdom is destroyed, which Jeremiah attributes to God's doing.

The second part of the request for justice is more severe. Here Jeremiah wants God to avenge Jacob—to act with vengeance against the nations that have destroyed Israel. This verse foreshadows events to come. Clearly Jeremiah here acts as Israel's intercessor *par excellence:*

> Pour out your wrath on the nations that do not know you
>   and on the peoples that do not call on your name;
> for they have devoured Jacob;
>   they have devoured him and consumed him,
>   and have laid waste his habitation. (v. 25)

The divine anger Jeremiah does not want to encounter, or have his community encounter, is the same anger that flames the divine wrath Jeremiah wants unleashed on the nations on account of their having destroyed Jacob/Israel. Jeremiah wants these villainous nations to meet their match and lose to one stronger than themselves: Israel's God. The inherent irony in verses 24-25 is this: in Jeremiah's time apostasy was apparently considered a far greater offense than a military invasion that captured people and land. The prophet's focus, and through the prophet the community's focus, is on the historical invasion and the unjust takeover of the land, and not on the weightier matters—the religious transgressions—that have deeply offended God. But as events unfold throughout the book of Jeremiah one sees that God's focus is primarily on the community, its apostasy and idolatry. It is for this that the community experiences God's anger. The Southern Kingdom is leveled. Only later do the nations receive their "just due" when they encounter God's divine anger and wrath (see Jer 46:1–51:58).

Jeremiah 11:18–12:6: "Why does the Way of the Guilty Prosper?"

In a reflective manner and tone, deeply conscious of himself and his God, Jeremiah continues to lament. This poem is the first in a series of formal lament songs found in the book of Jeremiah.[3] It consists of two major parts: 11:18-23 and 12:1-6. The first part, 11:18-23, contains two styles, poetry and prose, and can be subdivided into two units: a complaint by Jeremiah (11:18-20) and a divine response (11:21-23). The second part, like the first, is also a complaint (12:1-4) and a divine response (12:5-6). Together the two parts provide readers and listeners with a glimpse into the intimate and honest relationship shared between Jeremiah and God.

Jeremiah opens the first line of his lament with a reflection on God and the knowledge God gave him about his community: specifically, God showed Jeremiah the people's evil deeds. The double use of the root verb "to know" is a rhetorical technique known as *multiclimatum,* which Jeremiah uses quite frequently. It provides emphasis and often establishes some sort of relationship between ideas and character. In verse 18 the double use of "know" highlights the relationship that exists between God and Jeremiah as characters and with respect to revelation on God's part and the understanding, on Jeremiah's part, of what was revealed. Jeremiah "knew" certain things because God had made these things "known" to him, including his vocation

[3] See Jer 15:11-21; 17:14-18; 18:18-23; 20:7-18.

(see Jer 1:4-10) and the community's offenses, a knowledge that came with the call and mission to be a prophet.

The conjunction "but" in verse 19 signals a shift in thought. Here Jeremiah elaborates on the knowledge he did not have. Understanding himself to be somewhat "innocent" and perhaps a lot less "perceptive" than many of his community members, Jeremiah was unaware of the schemes people were plotting against him. The image of the gentle lamb led to slaughter that Jeremiah associates with himself metaphorically echoes Isaiah 53:7, the song of the Suffering Servant, where the same metaphor appears in relation to the Isaian servant and the suffering being borne on account of the prophetic vocation and mission. The reference here in Jeremiah suggests that he drifted along innocently within the community and "woke up" in the middle of his experience with them, only to discover that—to his surprise—they were devising schemes against him. This "delayed" knowledge is beneficial insofar as it can provide a person with an insider's view and firsthand knowledge of a situation before one's intuition and perception kick in to reveal the turning of tables and the preplanned plots in the making.

In the second half of verse 19 Jeremiah quotes his "enemies" and thus reveals their scheme: they want to kill him. The enemies' metaphorical reference to Jeremiah as a "tree" with "fruit" suggests how they view him: he is a person strong and vibrant, and they are threatened by him.

With the conjunction "but" in verse 20 Jeremiah shifts his and his audience's focus to God and expresses his desire for God to exert divine retribution on those plotting against him. He sees himself deserving of such a favor because he has "committed" his "cause" to God. He has been faithful to his God-given vocation and mission. Jeremiah's request is a classic example of the deuteronomistic theology of retribution that underlies much of the book of Jeremiah and that, historically, was probably part of the people's theological perspective, including Jeremiah's. Additionally, Jeremiah refers to God as "LORD of hosts," which suggests an image of power and military prowess, and he acknowledges God as someone who judges righteously and considers people carefully. For Jeremiah, God is powerful, righteous, astute, and just (v. 20).

God responds to the poet in verses 21-23. In a very personal message addressed to Jeremiah and directed at the people of Anathoth who seek Jeremiah's life because of his fidelity to his mission, God assures Jeremiah that the situation will be handled. The LORD of hosts responds:

> I am going to punish them; the young men shall die by the sword; their
> sons and their daughters shall die by famine; and not even a remnant

shall be left to them. For I will bring disaster upon the people of Anathoth, the year of their punishment.

God, the Sovereign One, the LORD of hosts, does answer Jeremiah's request and promise to act favorably on it.[4] As Walter Brueggemann notes:

> Beyond the vindication of the person of the prophet, this prayer and answer present a philosophy of history characteristic of prophetic faith. The men of Anathoth rejected a view of the historical process that asserted the end of the known world of royal-temple power. The divine response verifies such an establishment-ending word, however. It asserts that this prophetic word is authentic and enjoys the authorization and protection of the righteous Judge. What is guarded and endorsed here is not simply the person of the prophet, but the prophetic word that is indeed attested as the very word of Yahweh.[5]

The theological problem remains: God's justice is depicted as punitive, a reflection of one of the ways ancient people understood divine justice.

Jeremiah continues his conversation with God in 12:1-4. Here the poet puts his complaint before God in the form of a legal brief, which he constructs as a series of rhetorical questions and statements aimed at challenging God to be self-reflective on some of the divine ways that, to Jeremiah, make little sense. Before making his case he first affirms God and thus sets God up to be in a positive, listening posture:

> You will be in the right, O LORD,
>> when I lay charges against you;
>> but let me put my case to you.

So Jeremiah begins his case:

> Why does the way of the guilty prosper?
> Why do all who are treacherous thrive?
> You plant them, and they take root;
>> they grow and bring forth fruit;
> you are near in their mouths
>> yet far from their hearts. (v. 2)

---

[4] See Jer 15:19; 17:14 (2x); 20:7; 31:4, 18 (2x), and also Jack R. Lundbom, *Jeremiah 1–20.* AB 21A (New York: Doubleday, 1999) 636.

[5] Brueggemann, *Exile and Homecoming,* 117.

Jeremiah questions God's blessings on the wicked, especially when these people could not care less about God. Jeremiah here views the natural world with the eyes of a gardener. Together, the rhetorical questions and statements shed light on the character of God, who graces even the guilty and treacherous despite their state of being. Jeremiah's comments also shed light on his character: he is able to discern what is true and to see beyond the superficial and into the heart.

By means of a conjunction and personal address to God, Jeremiah shifts the focus and tone of his conversation, moving his audience from the legal to the intimate:

> But you, O Lord, know me;
> You see me and test me—my heart is with you. (v. 3a)

Jeremiah's words recall his call narrative, and here he reaffirms God's intimate knowledge of him. For Jeremiah, his relationship with his God is an affair of the heart. It is this bond with his God through the heart that enables him to remain faithful to God and to his people, to proclaim the harsh word when necessary, to feel God's pain and anguish and to be pained himself over his people's infidelity and offenses. Jeremiah's love is a suffering love that bears with and bears all.

Following these tender words, the prophet bellows out a request for divine retribution:

> Pull them out like sheep for the slaughter,
>   and set them apart for the day of slaughter. (v. 3b)

The simile of the sheep recalls Jeremiah 11:19. Jeremiah, who saw himself as like a lamb led to slaughter by his enemies, now wants God to lead the wicked to slaughter like sheep. Sheep, an image reflective of Israel's agrarian culture, were central to the nation's economy (cf. Gen 4:2) and were considered to be helpless animals in need of a shepherd to lead them. Here Jeremiah is not calling on God to "shepherd" the sheep but to act more like a warrior god—the Lord of hosts—who will prepare them to be sacrificed in the slaughter of battle. Implicit in Jeremiah's request to God is the idea of separation: "pull them out . . . set them apart for the day of slaughter." The phrases hint at the faithful remnant who will not be part of the fold that meets the sword on the day of slaughter and will thus survive the great battle.

Jeremiah returns to his legal brief in verse 4:

> How long will the land mourn,
>> and the grass of every field wither?
> For the wickedness of those who live in it
>> the animals and the birds are swept away,
>> and because people said, "He is blind to our ways."

With cosmological sweep Jeremiah illumines the devastation of the natural world by a severe drought, a sign of God's punitive justice foreshadowed in 11:22, where God promises that people will die by famine. Jeremiah links the wickedness of humanity to the suffering of the natural world. In essence it was thought in Jeremiah's time that God would strike the land and the animals in order to punish the wicked by taking away their food sources and supplies. By quoting the people, Jeremiah highlights their ignorance of God. Ironically, God is not blind to the people's ways, as they thought, and so divine chastisement has come upon them and, unfortunately, on the natural world as well.

As in 11:21-23, God responds to the poet's questions and comments, but instead of making promises God poses two questions to Jeremiah to make him think:

> If you have raced with foot-runners and they have wearied you,
>> how will you compete with horses?
> And if in a safe land you fall down,
>> how will you fare in the thickets of the Jordan? (v. 5)

Expecting, perhaps, no reply from Jeremiah other than for the prophet to engage in self-reflection for the purpose of finding strength within himself, God next offers Jeremiah insight and a piece of advice: his own family are his "enemies" and are out to get him; even if they should speak kindly to him, Jeremiah is to be on his guard against their verbal hypocrisy (v. 6).

In sum, Jeremiah's lament provides a glimpse of the dynamic relationship that exists between the prophet and his God, a relationship characterized by mutual respect, mutual attentiveness, and an underlying trust, so that Jeremiah is not afraid to ask some hard questions of his God, and God in turn is free enough, because of Jeremiah's trust and love, to challenge the prophet with other personal questions. Moreover, Jeremiah is revealed as someone fully committed to his God, to his vocation, and to his mission as a prophet in the midst of a people hostile toward him, including his own family and kinfolk. Jeremiah is God's prophet, and being of one heart and one mind, they continue to move forward together as Judah begins to collapse around them (see 12:7-17).

Jeremiah 15:15-21: Why is my Pain Unceasing?

> O LORD, you know;
>> remember me and visit me,
>> and bring down retribution for me on my persecutors. (v. 15a)

With sincerity and candor, and not without a bite, Jeremiah continues to lament to God. The first part of this prayer features Jeremiah as the speaker talking to God (vv. 15-18); the second part is God's reply to Jeremiah (vv. 19-21).

The poet-prophet begins his prayerful lament with a vocative, "O LORD," followed by a brief confession addressed to God, "you know," and a triple petition, "remember me," "visit me," "bring down retribution for me on my persecutors." What does God know? Although the text is obscure, Jeremiah has given those listening to his prayer an "insiders' view": God knows Jeremiah through and through from before his birth; God knows the fate of the people, which Jeremiah has tried repeatedly to warn them about; God knows Jeremiah's pain and the plotting of his adversaries; and God knows the future for the people after the exile. Jeremiah is aware that God has this breadth of knowledge and more, and what he seems to be implying here is: "God, you know my situation with my adversaries; deal with them." Appearing again as it has so often throughout the book of Jeremiah is the deuteronomistic theology of retribution. Interestingly enough, Jeremiah does not intend to defend himself; he wants God to do it on his behalf. Is Jeremiah expressing a lack of courage and prowess in the face of adversity, or is he trusting in the "LORD of hosts"? His plea continues:

> In your forbearance do not take me away;
>> know that on your account I suffer insult. (v. 15b)

This supplies additional information about Jeremiah and his view of God. While he trusts in God and has enough confidence to express his feelings honestly, Jeremiah also realize God's great power, and this knowledge, coupled with his expressed frustration and desire to have his adversaries dealt with, leads Jeremiah to remind God that he is bearing all this torment for God's sake. Thus even though Jeremiah repeatedly "complains" to God, he wants God to know that his complaining is justified. He does not want God to grow weary of his pining and sweep him away.

In verse 16 Jeremiah rejoices in God's words and being called by God's name. ("Jeremiah" means "YHWH has established.") This is ironic, since the word of God that Jeremiah must proclaim has, for the most part, been anything but positive and, we might add, Jeremiah is anything but an "establish-ment type"! Nevertheless, even the harshest word affords his listeners the opportunity to turn back to God. Jeremiah is the one who, being called by God's name, stands apart from his community even though he remains in the midst of it. He makes this point in verse 17:

> I did not sit in the company of merrymakers,
>   nor did I rejoice;
> under the weight of your hand I sat alone,
>   for you had filled me with indignation.

Chosen by God and distanced from his own, Jeremiah has experienced both delight and pain. The indignation inside Jeremiah is the prophetic passion that fuels his proclamation of God's word.

Jeremiah reveals the extent and depth of his pain through a rhetorical question to God:

> Why is my pain unceasing,
>   my wound incurable,
>   refusing to be healed? (v. 19)

Jeremiah's rhetorical question functions on several levels. First, it reveals the persistence of the insult and treachery of his "enemies"; second, it is God's pain that he bears—the wound the people have inflicted on God by their infidelity to both God and covenant relationship; third, it is the community's pain that he bears as a result of God's retribution. This "incurable wound," seen as God's purpose, will be the demise of the holy city, the Temple, and the Southern Kingdom of Judah. In essence the wound that cannot be cured, that refuses to be healed, is both the people's apostasy and offenses and the Babylonian invasion, all of which Jeremiah has to bear. This prompts him to exclaim:

> Truly, you are to me like a deceitful brook,
>   like waters that fail. (v. 18)

Jeremiah's simile suggests that God is *not* refreshing, healing, and restorative. All Jeremiah experiences from God is pain, and one wonders if behind his statements are not the questions "How have you made me a 'fortified city,' an 'iron pillar,' and a 'bronze wall' against the whole land?" "How have 'they' not prevailed against me?" "How have you delivered me?"

(see Jer 1:18-19). Such questions anticipate God's reply to Jeremiah in verses 19-21.

The conjunction "therefore" indicates a shift in Jeremiah's poem as well as a sense of sequence. God has listened to the prophet's lament and now offers a response that Jeremiah proclaims publicly and with authority: "Therefore thus says the LORD . . ." (v. 19a). God offers Jeremiah words of comfort and encouragement, and renews an earlier promise made to him in the context of his call and commissioning. Jeremiah again hears God's promise to be faithful to God's purposes. And how could God not remain faithful to Jeremiah? God is the God whose faithfulness is for all ages, but more importantly, Jeremiah has remained faithful to his God, to God's word, and to God's mission entrusted to him. The relationship between God and Jeremiah is mutual, and it bears witness to "covenant" whose binding cord is fidelity.

In sum, Jeremiah 15:15-21, as a lament addressed to God and answered by God, is a testimony to Jeremiah's "humanness" as he struggles to be faithful to his God and to his people in the midst of sheer frustration and pain. His vocation as God's prophet calls him to a certain "isolation," even though he remains in the presence of the community. He is a solitary singer of God's word, out there on the front line, taking the hits that come with being a "prophet." But he is not alone. God remains ever-present, listening, responding, encouraging, and faithful. God is Jeremiah's best friend, and Jeremiah is God's, too.

Jeremiah 17:14-18: Heal Me, O LORD

With profound confidence in his God and steadfast trust in God's justice and compassion, Jeremiah prays to God, begging God to heal him, save him, have mercy on him, and bring his persecutors to the day of their reckoning. Jeremiah 17:14-18 is another lament that reveals the contents of a poet-prophet's heart as it struggles in the midst of adversity.

Jeremiah opens his prayer with a double petition, asking for God's favor while simultaneously acknowledging his respect for God who is his "praise" (v. 4). In an attempt to bolster his request, he then makes God aware of his situation by quoting his adversaries who mock him and, indirectly, mock God: "Where is the word of the LORD? Let it come!" (v. 15). Jeremiah then reiterates to God his own fidelity and steadfastness to the tasks of his vocation, the courage he has demonstrated in not wishing for the "fatal day" that would end his labors and misery, and his frankness with God with respect to proclaiming God's word (v. 16). Having made a case for himself, Jeremiah petitions God again, acknowledging his dependence on God and God's help:

Do not become a terror to me;
>   you are my refuge in the day of disaster;
Let my persecutors be shamed,
>   but do not let me be shamed;
let them be dismayed,
>   but do not let me be dismayed;
bring on them the day of disaster;
>   destroy them with double destruction! (vv. 17-18)

Jeremiah prays for his own life to be spared while asking God to deal severely with his persecutors and thus relieve him of the pain and grief they are causing him. Jeremiah wants God to wipe out his persecutors. His four sequential requests for divine punishment emphasize this point, and the two counterparts to the first two petitions—"but do not let me be shamed . . . but do not let me be dismayed"—point up his desire to be exempt from the fate of his persecutors. His final phrase, "destroy them with double destruction!" captures his strong feelings toward his adversaries.

Jeremiah's poetic prayer reveals him as a man of great stamina whose strong relationship with God enables him to be direct, straightforward, and bold in his requests. Inherent in Jeremiah's prayer is a note of expectation. He expects his God to grant his requests because he has kept his end of the bargain. He has remained faithful to his God, and thus he can expect his God to be faithful to him.

Jeremiah 18:18-23: Give Heed to Me, O LORD

Jeremiah's adversaries are ruthless. They give him no peace and are persistent in their plots against him. Jeremiah's next prayer of lament combines both prose and poetry. As a composite unit verses 18-23 fall into two strophes: the plot against Jeremiah (vv. 18-20) and Jeremiah's petition for retribution (vv. 21-23).

Jeremiah's extended prose quotation provides a peek into the intention of the prophet's adversaries, who plot against him, resolve to accuse him falsely, and are determined to disregard his words (v. 19). The quotation sets the tone for the rest of the prayer, in which Jeremiah laments and makes his angry wishes known to God (vv. 20-23). Jeremiah begins his prayer to God with a petition that God will pay attention to him and to what his adversaries have just said (v. 19). He poses a challenge to God: "Is evil a recompense for good?" The frustrated prophet, knowing the wicked plots of his adversaries and his own fidelity, puts the question to God as if the two are face to face and nose to nose. Jeremiah answers his own question indirectly, with God listening in. His answer sheds light on the injustice of his situation: "Yet they have dug a pit for my life" (v. 20a). With God's attention now focused on his situation, Jeremiah attempts to jog God's memory with an emphatic imperative:

> Remember how I stood before you
> > to speak good for them,
> > to turn away your wrath from them. (v. 20b)

Jeremiah wants God to recall how he has been to this people who plot against him, and to make sure God realizes how unjustly he is being treated by his people. In telling God to "remember" the good he has done on behalf of this fickle people, Jeremiah is setting God up for his next request: justified divine retribution on his adversaries (vv. 21-23). "Therefore," because the people have acted wickedly, Jeremiah wants God to exercise divine justice on them as a form of chastisement. With a series of successive direct and indirect imperatives Jeremiah outlines for God what he wants God to do to his adversaries: strike them with famine, the sword, and pestilence. Essentially Jeremiah is urging God to let the Babylonian invasion begin. In verse 22b Jeremiah reiterates his reason for wanting such tragedies to take place: "For they have dug a pit to catch me, and snares for my feet" (v. 22b). He wants God to fight back for him and give these heartless people their "just due."

Jeremiah's tone softens in verse 23a. He expresses his confidence in God, affirming God's knowledge of the situation (you, O LORD, know . . .) while indirectly setting God up again to hear his next bold request:

> Do not forgive their iniquity,
> > do not blot out their sin from your sight.
> Let them be tripped up before you;
> > deal with them while you are angry.

Jeremiah is through with being nice to these people who are looking to trap him. He is angry with them, and in this posture he appeals to God's anger with them on account of their apostasy and idolatry; he says, "Go for it, God, go after them."

In turning against Jeremiah the people have lost their one advocate. They have willingly turned not only from God, but also from Jeremiah. This rejection should come as no surprise. Having fallen out of right relationship with their God, the people fall out of right relationship with those who embody the presence of God within the community. And having forsaken their God, how can they not try to put an end to one of God's prophets?

This passage also shows Jeremiah's skill, as he makes his verbal maneuvers to place God in a position of "listening," "remembering," and "knowing" in the hope that God will take his requests to heart and act on them. Not hearing a word from God, one wonders how God will respond. Although the people's fate has been foreshadowed many times, Jeremiah's prayer only asks that the inevitable take place. In that request, however, is an element of certitude. God and Jeremiah now desire the fate for this recalcitrant people. And so it will be.

Jeremiah 20:7-18: O LORD, You Have Duped Me . . .

The most poignant, profound, deeply passionate, and yet humorous of all Jeremiah's laments is this last one, Jeremiah 20:7-18. It is composed of two parts: a lament of an individual (vv. 7-13) and a curse (vv. 14-18). This lament illustrates both the rhetorical genius of Jeremiah as a poet and the passion and candor of Jeremiah as a prophet.

The first part of the lament can be subdivided into two parts: complaint (vv. 7-10) and praise (vv. 11-13). In verses 7-10 Jeremiah uses a series of rhetorical devices to communicate his feeling of being "betrayed" by God and to express to God the overwhelming fiery passion associated with the prophetic vocation that burns in his bones.

Jeremiah's rhetorical techniques include enjambment ("O LORD, you have duped me, and I was duped" [v. 1]),[6] metaphors ("I have become a laughingstock" [v. 7]; "For the word of the LORD has become to me a reproach and a derision all day long [v. 8]), simile ("then within me there is something like a burning fire" [v. 9]), a double entendre ("For whenever I speak, I must cry out, I must shout, 'Violence and destruction!'" [v. 8]), and quoted statements ("For I hear many whispering: 'Terror is all around! Denounce him! Let us denounce him!' All my close friends are watching for me to stumble. 'Perhaps he can be enticed, and we can prevail against him, and take our revenge on him'" [v. 10]). With graphic images Jeremiah describes his harrowing experience, filled with adversity and yet also with energy. Even though he suffers the pain of thinking God has tricked him and overpowered him to the extent of bringing him low in the eyes of his community, as opposed to becoming a fortified city, iron pillar, and bronze wall as God had promised (see Jer 1:18), Jeremiah cannot turn away from his God and the prophetic task entrusted to him. He must proclaim his God and

---

[6] The Hebrew root *pth* can either be translated "to entice" or "to dupe." In light of the content of Jer 1:17-19, I choose to interpret the verb as "dupe," and not, as the NRSV suggests, "entice."

speak in God's name, for God's spirit is stronger than Jeremiah's will and desire, and God's word cannot be restrained. This "violence and destruction" that Jeremiah cries out is both the violence and destruction the community is doing and the violence and destruction yet to come with the Babylonian invasion. Jeremiah's double entendre is both an indictment and a fore-shadowing of future events. At this point Jeremiah's closest friends have become his adversaries, and they are thirsting for his blood.

Given such circumstances, one would imagine that Jeremiah would want to run and hide somewhere, or to give himself altogether into the hands of his enemies and thus have his pain ended once and for all, despite that burning spirit in his bones. But he cannot do any of those things. His faith in his God is too strong; he proclaims his trust and begs for God's help:

> But the LORD is with me like a dread warrior;
> > therefore my persecutors will stumble,
> > and they will not prevail.
> They will be greatly shamed,
> > for they will not succeed.
> Their eternal dishonor
> > will never be forgotten.
> O LORD of hosts, you test the righteous,
> > you see the heart and the mind;
> let me see your retribution upon them,
> > for to you I have committed my cause. (vv. 11-12)

Jeremiah stands confident, bolstered by the profound realization that his God is with him as a "warrior god," and together they will fight against Jeremiah's persecutors and overpower them. For the first time Jeremiah does not ask God to fight his battles for him. He and God are going to work to-gether, and together they will succeed. Verse 11 speaks of a beautiful union between the prophet and God, a union characteristic of the prophetic voca-tion and mission. Still, verse 12 reveals Jeremiah's "humanness." The voca-tive, "O LORD of hosts," indicates a shift in tone and focus. As so often before, Jeremiah talks with God directly. He affirms his God and beckons God to act with retributive justice against his enemies, and he reaffirms his own commitment to God and to the task at hand (v. 12).

After petitioning God, Jeremiah bursts into song:

> Sing to the LORD;
> > praise the LORD!
> For he has delivered the life of the needy
> > from the hands of evildoers. (v. 13)

Whether or not Jeremiah realizes it, this song foreshadows his own fate. He will be delivered from the hands of evildoers—his own personal adversaries and the Babylonians. Captured by the invaders, he will escape from his enemies, and in exile he will evade the fate of so many of his people. Jeremiah will live on and prevail, and God's promise to him will be fulfilled. This song, however, is not just a personal one. It is also a communal song of praise that offers a vision of hope for some members within Jeremiah's community. Like Jeremiah, those who have remained faithful—the remnant —will be delivered from the hands—the swords—of those who will invade their land. These faithful ones will also be delivered from the wickedness of some of those among their own people. For all the faithful, the exile will be a means to life.

The last part of Jeremiah's lament (vv. 14-18) is a curse that has brought mixed reviews from scholars who generally tend to hear Jeremiah's voice as suicidal and representative of one who has sunk into deep depression. Jeremiah's rhetoric could certainly lead one to draw such conclusions. But if we hear verses 14-18 in the context of 7-13, Jeremiah's expressed confidence in God and his song of praise, we may think that Jeremiah is being ironically humorous in verses 14-18. Given all that he has had to proclaim, do, endure, see, and bear up against, it is no wonder that he curses the day he was born. It is as if he is saying, after a long and trying day of trials and tribulations, "Why did I get out of bed this morning?" We should note that Jeremiah curses the day he was born; he does not curse his parents, because to do so would be an offense. His final words are the most ironic of all:

> Why did I come forth from the womb
> to see toil and sorrow,
> and spend my days in shame? (v. 18)

Jeremiah has seen toil and sorrow and has spent his days in shame. But he also came forth from the womb to be a word of hope, a sign of God's enduring presence even in the midst of a community's bleakest moments.

What Jeremiah sees through his eyes is all that is ugly around him; what Jeremiah's later audiences see as they view Jeremiah the character is all that is human, but all that is divine as well, with Jeremiah the embodiment of wholeness and holiness. Whether or not Jeremiah's primary audience saw through Jeremiah to behold the presence of God among them remains a mystery, for both the text and Jeremiah focus only on those members within the community who verbalized opposition to God and the prophet. Would that an alternative voice might come into focus and emerge from the silence! One last point: verse 13, Jeremiah's song of praise, which is often considered secondary, is situated at the center of verses 7-18. At the heart of the prophetic tradition, and central to it, is a word of hope.

In Retrospect . . .

Jeremiah's conversation with God, in the form of poetic laments and prayers, captures the dynamic of his inner life and reveals the true beauty of his character amid the sordidness of his own people. God's responses to Jeremiah bear witness to the fact that God does listen and respond to the stirrings of one's heart, both in its agony and in its ecstasy. Furthermore, the relationship that Jeremiah and God share sheds light on the life of a prophet, revealing to later audiences that the life and spirit of both the prophet and God are intimately woven—wedded—together without erasing their own voices and personal distinctiveness. Although Jeremiah and God share a special bond that bespeaks union, both are seen as distinct characters throughout these texts and the book as whole. Finally, Jeremiah's poetic conversations with and to God are not just poems. They tell stories about historical events past, present, and yet to come, and they remind listeners and readers today that one like Jeremiah—God's poet and storyteller—continues to live at the heart of all, trying to sing.

EPILOGUE

Before I formed you in the womb I knew you,
and before you were born I consecrated you;
I appointed you a prophet to the nations. (Jer 1:5)

To be known intimately by someone can be a wonderful, freeing, and comforting experience, especially when such knowledge is in the context of a mutually caring and respectful relationship. At the same time, however, the experience of being "known" can also be unsettling and disconcerting, for to be "known" is to become vulnerable. And to be "appointed" to do a certain task, especially when that task has an important and global aspect to it, can be both a challenging and a rewarding experience, particularly for a person who is "young" in age. To be "known" and "appointed" *by God* is an experience that will take a lifetime to understand and live out. Such was the experience of Jeremiah, who, "known" and "appointed" by God, had the awesome task of delivering a vision, a message to his listeners—a message that would expose their sinfulness and foreshadow the eventual loss of their homeland, their holy city Jerusalem, and God's holy dwelling place, the Temple. The Babylonians, a fearful and awesome people of tremendous power, would eventually invade Judah and devastate the land and its people. And Jeremiah knew it and lived to see his vision and message fulfilled. No wonder he blurted out:

Cursed be the day
    on which I was born!
The day when my mother bore me,
    let it not be blessed!
Cursed be the man
    who brought the news to my father, saying,
"A child is born to you, a son,"
    making him very glad.
Let that man be like the cities
    that the LORD overthrew without pity;

let him hear a cry in the morning
  and an alarm at noon,
because he did not kill me in the womb;
  so my mother would have been my grave,
  and her womb forever great.
Why did I come forth from the womb
  to see toil and sorrow
  and spend my days in shame? (20:14-18)

The answer to Jeremiah's question is a simple one: he came forth from the womb—"known," "consecrated," and "appointed" by God—so that he could be a sign of God's faithful love for his own people, and an inspiration to those of us today who can identify with his person, his spirit, his great love for God and his community, and his unpopular task of having to say a word that "cuts to the bone" to expose injustice and point the way back to right relationship with God, with one another, with all creation. The character Jeremiah, interfacing with his God, his community, his historical and social times and events, shows us that the task of a prophet is not to be successful, but rather to be faithful—faithful to God, faithful to one's people, and faithful to the vocation of being a prophet no matter what the cost. Through his proclamations and his conversations with God, Jeremiah also shows us that despite people's infidelity to God—their apostate and idolatrous ways, their disregard for covenant relationship that calls them to act justly, love tenderly, and walk humbly with God (cf. Mic 6:8)—God will remain faithful to the people through the presence of the prophet who continually calls the community to "repent," "reform," "turn back."

Perhaps most importantly, Jeremiah teaches us that whoever would be a prophet must be ready for the experience of pain and suffering that comes from experiencing human injustice, feeling God's pain and suffering at such injustice, and being subjected to the pain and suffering associated not only with being rejected by one's own community because one has taken a stand against injustice by exposing it, but also with seeing how a person's violation of right relationship can lead to his or her own demise and that of others. Jeremiah shows us that the prophet has no control over people; the prophet can only offer encouragement and hope for a change of behavior, a change of heart within a struggling community. Finally, Jeremiah shows us that in order to bear such pain and suffering while remaining faithful to God and God's people, the prophet has to "let go" to God completely, knowing that God continues to work within the human condition as well as within creation, to bring about transformation into wholeness, holiness, and peace.

Jeremiah, preacher of grace and poet of truth, invites us to journey with God, to listen for God's invitation to act prophetically in daily life, and to embrace that invitation wholeheartedly again and again so that, with those who have gone before us, we too can be a sign of hope and a ray of light in a world that aches for justice, right relationship, and abiding peace.

> See, today I appoint *you* over nations and over kingdoms,
>> to pluck up and to pull down,
>> to destroy and to overthrow,
>> to build and to plant. (1:10)

SELECTED BIBLIOGRAPHY

Ackerman, Susan. *Under Every Green Tree: Popular Religion in Sixth-Century Judah*. Atlanta: Scholars Press, 1992.

Alter, Robert. *The Art of Biblical Poetry*. New York: Basic Books, 1985.

Balentine, Samuel E. "The Prophet as Intercessor: A Reassessment," *Journal of Biblical Literature* 103 (1984) 161–73.

Bauer, Angela. *Gender in the Book of Jeremiah: A Feminist-Literary Reading*. Studies in Biblical Literature 5. Ed. Hemchand Gossia. New York: Peter Lang, 1999.

Baumgartner, Walter. *Jeremiah's Poems of Lament*. Tr. David E. Orton. Sheffield: Almond Press, 1988.

Berquist, Jon. L. "Prophet Legitimation in Jeremiah," *Vetus Testamentum* 39 (1989) 129–39.

Black, Sheldon H. *Rhetorical Criticism: A Study in Method*. New York: Macmillan, 1965.

Blenkinsopp, Joseph. "Stylistics of Old Testament Poetry," *Biblica* 44 (1963) 352–58.

Booth, Wayne C. *A Rhetoric of Irony*. Chicago: University of Chicago Press, 1974.

Bracke, John M. *Jeremiah 1–29*. Westminster Bible Companion. Louisville: Westminster John Knox, 2000.

———. *Jeremiah 30–52 and Lamentations*. Westminster Bible Companion. Louisville: Westminster John Knox, 2000.

Bright, John. *Jeremiah*. Anchor Bible 21. Garden City, NY: Doubleday, 1965.

———. *A History of Israel*. 4th ed. Louisville: Westminster John Knox, 2000.

Brueggemann, Walter. *To Pluck Up, to Tear Down: A Commentary on the Book of Jeremiah 1–25*. Grand Rapids: Eerdmans, 1988.

———. *To Build, To Plant: A Commentary on Jeremiah 26–52*. Grand Rapids: Eerdmans, 1991.

———. *A Commentary on Jeremiah: Exile and Homecoming*. Grand Rapids: Eerdmans, 1998.

Carroll, Robert P. *Jeremiah*. Old Testament Library. Philadelphia: Westminster, 1986.

Clements, Ronald E. *Jeremiah*. Interpretation. Atlanta: John Knox, 1988.

Craigie, Peter C., Page H. Kelley, and Joel F. Drinkard, Jr. *Jeremiah 1–25*. Word Biblical Commentary. Dallas: Word Books, 1991.

De Moor, Johannes C. *The Elusive Prophet: The Prophet as a Historical Person, Literary Character and Anonymous Artist.* Oudtestamentische Studien XLV. Leiden: Brill, 2001.

Diamond, A. R. *The Confessions of Jeremiah in Context: Scenes of Prophetic Drama.* JSOTSup 45. Sheffield: JSOT Press, 1987.

Diamond, A. R. Pete, Kathleen M. O'Connor, and Louis Stulman, eds. *Troubling Jeremiah.* JSOTSup 260. Sheffield: Sheffield Academic Press, 1999.

Fretheim, Terence E. *Jeremiah.* Smyth & Helwys Bible Commentary. Macon: Smyth & Helwys Publishing, Inc., 2002.

———. "The Repentance of God: A Study of Jeremiah 18:7-10," *Hebrew Annual Review* 11 (1987) 81–92.

Fritz, Volkmar, Karl-Friedrich Pohlmann, and Hans-Christoph Schmitt. *Prophet und Prophetenbuch.* New York: Walter de Gruyter, 1989.

Gitay, Yehoshua. "Rhetorical Criticism and the Prophetic Discourse," *Journal for the Study of the New Testament* 50 (1991) 13–24.

Greenwood, David C. "On the Jewish Hope for a Restored Northern Kingdom," *Zeitschrift für die alttestamentliche Wissenschaft* 88 (1976) 376–85.

Heschel, Abraham Joshua. "Prophetic Inspiration: An Analysis of Prophetic Consciousness," *Judaism* 11 (1962) 3–13.

Holladay, William L. *Jeremiah: A Fresh Reading.* New York: Pilgrim, 1990.

———. *Jeremiah 1.* Hermeneia. Philadelphia: Fortress Press, 1986.

———. *Jeremiah 2.* Hermeneia. Philadelphia: Fortress Press, 1989.

Huffmon, Herbert B. "The Impossible: God's Words of Assurance in Jer 31:35-37," in Stephen L. Cook and Sara C. Winter, eds., *On The Way to Nineveh: Studies in Honor of George M. Landes.* Atlanta: Scholars Press, 1999.

Jansen, J. Gerald. *Studies in the Text of Jeremiah.* Cambridge: Harvard University Press, 1993.

Jones, Douglas R. *Jeremiah.* New Century Bible Commentary. Grand Rapids: Eerdmans, 1992.

Keown, Gerald L., Pamela L. Scalise, and Thomas G. Smothers. *Jeremiah 26–52.* Word Biblical Commentary. Dallas: Word Books, 1995.

Lalleman-De Winkel, Hetty. *Jeremiah in Prophetic Tradition: An Examination of the Book of Jeremiah in the Light of Israel's Prophetic Traditions.* Leuven: Peeters, 2000.

Leota, Peniamina. "For the Right of Possession and Redemption is Yours; Buy it for Yourself," *Pacific Journal of Theology* 22 (1999) 59–65.

Lewin, Ellen Davis. "Arguing for Authority: A Rhetorical Study of Jeremiah 1:4-19 and 20:7-18," *Journal for the Study of the Old Testament* 32 (1985) 105–119.

Lundbom, Jack R. "Jeremiah 15:15-21 and the Call of Jeremiah," *Scandinavian Journal for the Old Testament* 9 (1995) 143–55.

———. *Jeremiah: A Study in Ancient Hebrew Rhetoric.* 2nd ed. Winona Lake: Eisenbrauns, 1997.

———. *Jeremiah 1–20.* Anchor Bible 21A. New York: Doubleday, 1999.

————. *Jeremiah 21–36*. Anchor Bible 21B. New York: Doubleday, 2004.

————. *Jeremiah 37–52*. Anchor Bible 21C. New York: Doubleday, 2004.

May, Herbert G. "The Ten Lost Tribes," *Biblical Archaeologist* 6 (1943) 55–60.

McKeating, Henry. *The Book of Jeremiah*. Peterborough: Epworth Press, 1999.

Nasuti, Harry P. "A Prophet to the Nations: Diachronic and Synchronic Readings of Jeremiah 1," *Hebrew Annual Review* 10 (1987) 249–66.

O'Connor, Kathleen M. *The Confessions of Jeremiah: Their Interpretation and Role in Chapters 1–25*. SBL Dissertation Series. Atlanta: Scholars Press, 1988.

Parke-Taylor, Geoffrey H. *The Formation of the Book of Jeremiah: Doublets and Recurring Phrases*. SBLMS 51. Atlanta: Society of Biblical Literature, 2000.

Pixley, Jorge. *Jeremiah*. Chalice Commentaries for Today. St. Louis: Chalice Press, 2004.

Powell, Mark Alan. *What is Narrative Criticism?* Guides to Biblical Scholarship. Minneapolis: Fortress Press, 1990.

Rhodes, Arnold B. "Israel's Prophets as Intercessors," in Arthur L. Merrill and Thomas W. Overholt, eds., *Scripture in History & Theology: Essays in Honor of J. Coert Rylaasdam*. Pittsburgh: Pickwick Press, 1977.

Rayappan, Arasakumar. *The Divine Struggle: Divine-Cosmic-Human Relationship in Je IX*. European University Studies 740, Series XXIII: Theology. New York: Peter Lang, 2001.

Rudolph, Wilhelm. *Jeremiah*. Handbuch zum Alten Testament. Tübingen: J.C.B. Mohr [Paul Siebeck], 1968.

Smith, Mark S. *The Laments of Jeremiah and Their Contexts: A Literary and Redactional Study of Jeremiah 11–20*. SBLMS 42. Atlanta: Scholars Press, 1990.

Stulman, Louis. *Jeremiah*. Abingdon Old Testament Commentaries. Nashville: Abingdon, 2005.

Thompson, J. Arthur. *The Book of Jeremiah*. New International Commentary on the Old Testament. Grand Rapids: Eerdmans, 1980.

Trible, Phyllis. *Rhetorical Criticism: Context, Method, and the Book of Jonah*. Guides to Biblical Scholarship. Minneapolis: Fortress Press, 1994.

Youngblood, Ronald. "The Call of Jeremiah," *Criswell Theological Review* 5.1 (1990) 99–108.

Volz, Paul. *Der Prophet Jeremia*. Kommentar zum Alten Testament. Leipzig: Deichert, 1928; 3rd ed. Tübingen: Mohr, 1930.

Westermann, Claus. *Prophetic Oracles of Salvation in the Old Testament*. Tr. Keith Crim. Louisville: Westminster John Knox, 1991.

Weiser, Artur. *Das Buch des Propheten Jeremia*. Altes Testament Deutsch. Göttingen: Vandenhoeck & Ruprecht, 1969.

INDEX OF AUTHORS
AND PROPER NAMES

INDEX OF BIBLICAL CITATIONS

INDEX OF TOPICS